Sunny Amigurumi

7 Daffodil Spring Fairy
15 Flowers & Bugs
21 Rainbow Flower
27 Sunflower
32 Four Seasons Birds
37 Easter Bears
43 Sweet Fairy
48 Bride & Groom
57 Cute Couple
64 Heart Cushion
67 Flower Princess
72 Rainbow Girl

76 How to join Yarn
76 How to read pattern
76 Comparison color chart for Catania & DMC Pera No3
77 Yarn Weight System
77 Crochet Hook Conversion Chart

From the series : Sayjai's Amigurumi Crochet Patterns, volume 4
K and J Publishing, 16 Whitegate Close, Swavesey, Cambridge CB24 4TT, England

7

15

21

27

32

37

43

48

57

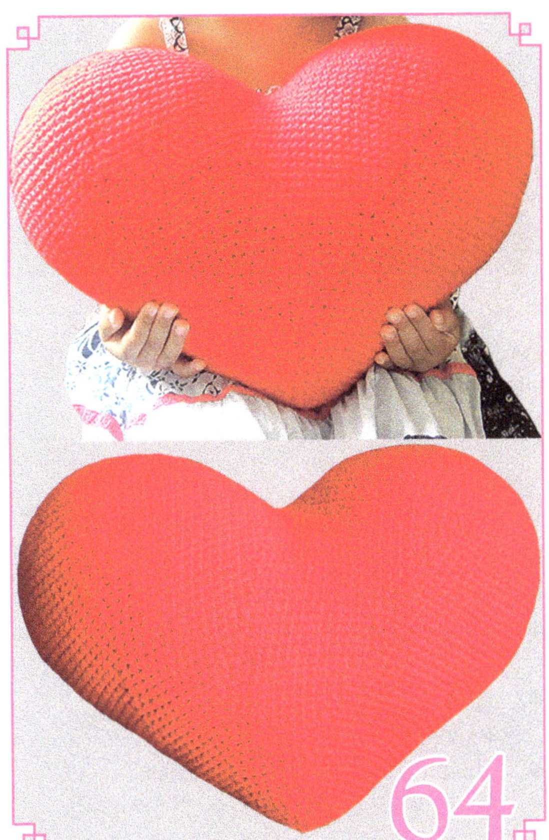
64

67

72

Introduction

Sunny Amigurumi is a collection of cute and happy crochet patterns. You need a basic knowledge of crochet to read the patterns.

Size:

You can make the doll smaller or bigger by using different yarn and hook, without changing a pattern.

- The small dolls are 2 to 10 inches/ 5 to 25 cm high.
- The Big Flowers are 16 inches/ 40 cm high.
- The Heart Cushion is 16 inches/ 40 cm wide and 11 inches/ 27.5 cm tall.

The size of the doll depends on the size of the crochet hook, the thickness of yarn and how you stuff it; a bigger hook and thicker yarn make a bigger doll. A doll stuffed tightly is bigger than a loose stuffed doll.

Yarn:

Small dolls & flowers: use No 2 yarn (Sport, Baby)

- Catania yarn from Schachenmayr SMC or use DMC Petra No 3 (the comparison color chart for Catania & DMC Petra on page 76)

- For 4 ply Acrylic yarn, you can use cotton yarn: Catania yarn from Schachenmayr SMC or DMC Petra No3 .

  You can also use No 3 yarn (DK, Light Worsted) with 3.5 - 4 mm hook.

Heart Cushion use No 5 yarn (Bulky, Chunky)

- Robin Chunky yarn

Abbreviations

This book uses USA crochet terminology.

ch = chain
sc = single crochet
hdc = half double crochet
dc = double crochet
st = stitch
sl = slip
rnd = round
tog = together

Conversion chart for USA/ UK crochet abbreviations:

USA Crochet Abbreviations	UK Crochet Abbreviations
sc = single crochet	dc = double crochet
hdc = half double crochet	htr = half treble crochet
dc = double crochet	tr = treble crochet

For the first round: you can do 6 sc in magic ring instead of "Ch 2, 6 sc in second chain from hook."

Daffodil Spring Fairy

Materials

For 4 flowers, fairy and watering can.

- Heavy Worsted Weight* (falls between an aran and a chunky weight or between No 4 and No 5 yarn) Rowan Cotton Rope; Limeade shade 65 (green) = 50 g
- 5 mm hook (US = H, UK = 6) for watering can

*You can use these yarns instead of Rowan Cotton Rope:

1. No 3 yarn 3 light (DK, Light Worsted) crochet 2 strands together with a 5 mm hook.

2. No 2 yarn 2 fine (Sport, Baby) crochet 3 strands together with a 5 mm hook (Catania yarn from Schachenmayr SMC or Petra No3)

- No 2 yarn (Sport, Baby) 2 fine
  Catania yarn from Schachenmayr SMC; Light yellow = 40 g, Dark yellow = 30 g, Cream = 5 g, Green = 5 g and a little bit of Red for embroider mouth
- 3.25 mm hook (US = D, UK = 10)
- Tapestry needle
- Two Black 4 mm beads for eyes or other eyes as desired
- Sewing needle and thread for attaching eyes
- Polyester fiberfill = 10 g
- Iron wire (florist wire 18 gauge) for the stem of Daffodil (5"/13 cm for one flower stem. You can use any length.)
- Pliers for cutting and bending the wire
- All purpose glue

Sizes

The Fairy is 2 inches (5 cm) high (sitting). The Daffodil flower is 1.5 inches (3.8 cm) tall, excluding stem.
Watering can diameter: 3 inches (7.5 cm), tall: 3 inches (7.5 cm)

Watering Can

Note

- Container and spout are beginning each round with chain(s) and join at the end of round.
- Handle is working in continuous rounds, do not join or turn.
- Mark first stitch of each round.
- Use Rowan Cotton Rope yarn and a 5 mm hook.

Container

Rnd 1: Ch 2, 6 sc in second chain from hook, join with sl st in first st. (6)
Rnd 2: Ch 1, 2 sc in each st around, join with sl st in first st. (12)
Rnd 3: Ch 1, sc in same st, 2 sc in next st, (sc in next st, 2 sc in next st) 5 times, join with sl st in first st. (18)
Rnd 4: Ch 1, sc in same st, 2 sc in next st, (sc in next 2 sts, 2 sc in next st) 5 times, sc in next st, join with sl st in first st. (24)
Rnd 5: Ch 1, sc in same st, sc in next 2 sts, 2 sc in next st, (sc in next 3 sts, 2 sc in next st) 5 times, join with sl st in first st. (30)
Rnd 6: Ch 1, sc in same st, sc in next st, 2sc in next st, (sc in next 4 sts, 2sc in next st) 5 times, sc in next 2 sts, join with sl st in first st. (36)
Rnd 7: Working in back loops only. Ch 1, sc in each st around, join with sl st in first st. (36)
Rnd 8-18: Ch 1, sc in each st around, join with sl st in first st. (36)
Rnd 19: Sl st in each st around, fasten off. (36)

Spout

Rnd 1: Ch 2, 6 sc in second chain from hook, join with sl st in first st. (6)

Rnds 2-4 are working in back loops only.
Rnd 2: Ch 1, 2 sc in each st around, join with sl st in first st. (12)
Rnd 3: Ch 1, sc in same st, 2 sc in next st, (sc in next st, 2 sc in next st) 5 times, join with sl st in first st. (18)
Rnd 4: Ch 1, sc first 2 sts tog, sc in next st, (sc next 2 sts tog, sc in next st) 5 times, join with sl st in first st. (12)

Rnd 5: Ch 1, sc first 2 sts tog, sc next 2 sts tog around, join with sl st in first st. Stuff. (6)
Rnd 6-10: Ch 1, sc in each st around, join with sl st in first st. (6)
Rnd 11: Ch 3(count as one dc), 2 dc in same st, hdc in next st, sc in next st, sl st in next st, sc in next st, hdc in next st, join with sl st in first st. Leave long end for sewing, fasten off. Stuff. (8)

Edge of rose
Join yarn to free loop on rnd 3, sl st around, fasten off.

Handle
Do not stuff the handle.

Rnd 1: Ch 2, 5 sc in second chain from hook. (5)

Rnd 2-19: Sc in each st around. (5)

Rnd 20: Sc in each st around, join with sl st in first st. Leave long end for sewing, fasten off. (5)

Finishing
Sew rnd 1 of handle on rnds 17-18 of container.

Sew rnds 18-19 of handle to rows 7-8 of container.

Pin spout opposite the handle, rows 11 of spout (the dc sts on the bottom) on rows 8-11 of container.

Fairy

Use No 2 yarn (Catania or Petra No3) and 3.25 mm hook.

Head and Body

Work from bottom of the body to top of the head.

Rnd 1: With **Dark yellow** (dress color), ch 5, sc in second chain from hook, sc in next 2 chs, 3 sc in next ch; working in remaining loops on opposite side of chain, sc in next 2 chs, 2 sc in next ch. (10)

	x	x	x	x	o
x	o	o	o	o	x
	x	x	x	x	

o = chain x = sc

Rnd 2: 2 sc in next st, sc in next 2 sts, 2 sc in next 3 sts, sc in next 2 sts, 2 sc in next 2 sts. (16)
Rnd 3: (Sc in next 7 sts, 2 sc in next st) 2 times. (18)
Rnd 4: Sc in each st around. (18)
Rnd 5: (Sc next 2 sts tog, sc in next st) around. (12)
Rnd 6: Working in back loops only. (Sc next 2 sts tog, sc in next 2 sts) around, changing to **Cream** (skin color) in last 2 loops of last st. Stuff. (9)
Rnd 7: 2 sc in each st around. (18)
Rnd 8: (Sc in next 2 sts, 2 sc in next st) around. (24)
Rnd 9: (Sc in next 7 sts, 2 sc in next st) around. (27)
Rnd 10-14: Sc in each st around. (27)
Rnd 15: (Sc next 2 sts tog, sc in next st) around. Stuff. (18)
Rnd 16: (Sc next 2 sts tog, sc in next st) around. (12)
Rnd 17: Sc next 2 sts tog around, join with sl st in first st, fasten off. (6)

Dress

Rnd 1: Join **Dark yellow** to free loop on rnd5, ch 3 (count as one dc), dc in next 2 sts, 2 dc in next st, (dc in next 3 sts, 2 dc in next st) 2 times, join with sl st in first st. (15)
Rnd 2: Ch 3 (count as one dc), dc in next 3 sts, 2 dc in next st, (dc in next 4 sts, 2 dc in next st) 2 times, join with sl st in first st. (18)
Rnd 3: Ch 3 (count as one dc), dc in next 4 sts, 2 dc in next st, (dc in next 5 sts, 2 dc in next st) 2 times, join with sl st in first st. (21)
Rnd 4: Ch 1, sc in same st, (ch 2, sc in next st) around, join with sl st in first st, fasten off.

Arm

Make 2, do not stuff arms.

Rnd 1: With **Cream**, ch 2, 5 sc in second chain from hook. (5)
Rnd 2-3: Sc in each st around. (5)
Rnd 4: Sc in each st around, join with sl st in first st. Leave long end for sewing, fasten off. (5)

Sew arms to body on rnd 6.

Leg

Make 2, do not stuff legs.

Rnd 1: With **Cream**, ch 2, 6 sc in second chain from hook. (6)
Rnd 2-4: Sc in each st around. (6)
Rnd 5: Sc in each st around, join with sl st in first st. Leave long end for sewing, fasten off. (6) Sew legs to body on rnd 2.

Flower cap

Start from the top of cap.

Rnd 1: With **Light yellow**, ch 2, 6 sc in second chain from hook. (6)
Rnd 2: 2 sc in each st around. (12)
Rnd 3: (Sc in next st, 2 sc in next st) around. (18)
Rnd 4: (2 sc in next st, sc in next st) around. (27)

Petals

Working in rows.

First Petal

Row 5: 2 sc in next st, sc in next 2 sts, 2 sc in next st, turn. (6)
Row 6-9: Ch 1, sc in each st across, turn. (6)
Row 10: Ch 1, sc first 2 sts tog, (sc next 2 sts tog) 2 times, turn. (3)
Row 11: Ch 1, sc first 2 sts tog, sc in next st, turn. (2)
Row 12: Ch 1, sc first 2 sts tog; working in ends of rows, sl st in next 8 rows (end of rows 12-5), sl st in next free loop of rnd 4.

Second Petal

Row 5: Ch 1, 2 sc in first st, sc in next 3 sts, 2 sc in next st, turn. (7)
Row 6-9: Ch 1, sc in each st across, turn. (7)
Row 10: Ch 1, sc first 2 sts tog, (sc next 2 sts tog) 2 times, sc in next st, turn. (4)
Row 11: Ch 1, sc first 2 sts tog, sc next 2 sts tog, turn. (2)
Row 12: Ch 1, sc first 2 sts tog, turn; working in ends of rows, sl st in next 8 rows (end of rows 12-5), sl st in next free loop of rnd 4.

Third Petal

Row 5: Ch 1, 2 sc in first st, sc in next 2 sts, 2 sc in next st, turn. (6)
Row 6-9: Ch 1, sc in first st, sc in each st across, turn. (6)
Row 10: Ch 1, sc first 2 sts tog, (sc next 2 sts tog) 2 times, turn. (3)
Row 11: Ch 1, sc first 2 sts tog, sc in next st, turn. (2)
Row 12: Ch 1, sc first 2 sts tog, turn; working in ends of rows, sl st in next 8 rows (end of rows 12-5), sl st in next free loop of rnd 4.

Fourth and Sixth Petals

Do the same as second petal.

Fifth Petal

Do the same as third petal.

Picture of finished Flower cap.

Put the flower cap on the head and sew.

Finishing

Sew eyes 5 sts apart between rnds 11-12. With **Red** yarn, embroider mouth on rnd 10.

Daffodil Flower

Use No 2 yarn (Catania or Petra No3) and 3.25 mm hook.

Flower

Rnd 1: With **Light yellow**, ch 2, 6 sc in second chain from hook. (6)

Rnd 2: (Sc in next st, 2 sc in next st) around. (9)

Rnd 3-4: Sc in each st around. (9)

Rnd 5: (2 sc in next st, sc in next 2 sts) around, changing to **Dark yellow** in last 2 loops of last st. (12)

See pictures for how to change yarn color below.

Put **light yellow** over the work and leave it (do not cut, we will use it to make petals later.) then change to **Dark yellow**.

Rnd 6: Working in back loops only. Sc in each st around. (12)
Rnd 7: Sc in each st around. (12)
Rnd 8: (Sc in next 3 sts, 2 sc in next st) around. (15)
Rnd 9: Sc in each st around. (15)
Rnd 10: (Sc in next 4 sts, 2 sc in next st) around. (18)
Rnd 11: Sc in each st around. (18)
Rnd 12: (Ch 2, sl st in next st) around, fasten off.

Petals Continue working with **Light yellow** yarn. Working in rows.

First Petal
Row 6: Working in free loops of rnd 5. Ch 1, 2 sc in same st, 2 sc in next st, turn. (4)
Row 7-9: Ch 1, sc in each st across, turn. (4)
Row 10: Ch 1, sc first 2 sts tog, sc next 2 sts tog, turn. (2)

Row 11: Ch 1, sc first 2 sts tog; working in ends of rows, sl st in next 6 rows (end of rows 11-6), sl st in next free loop of rnd 5.

Second – Sixth Petals
Row 6: Ch 1, 2 sc in same st, 2 sc in next st, turn. (4)
Row 7-9: Ch 1, sc in each st across, turn. (4)
Row 10: Ch 1, sc first 2 sts tog, sc next 2 sts tog, turn. (2)
Row 11: Ch 1, sc first 2 sts tog, turn; working in ends of rows, sl st in next 6 rows (end of rows 11-6), sl st in next free loop of rnd 5.

Pictures of finished flower.

Stamens and Stem

Cut 2 pieces of light yellow yarn 2 inches long, fold the yarn in half and loop an iron wire around the center and squeeze the wire.

Put the wire through the flower.

Use needle to get green yarn through one stitch of rnd 1 of flower.

Put glue around bottom of flower. Wrap the yarn around up to the bottom of flower continuously for 0.1-0.2" (0.5cm) then wrap the yarn around down the stem, put glue around the wire at the end of the stem. See pictures.

Flowers & Bugs

Materials

- No 2 yarn (Sport, Baby) 2 fine 4 ply Acrylic yarn; Cream = 5 g, Green = 10 g, Pink = 5 g, Yellow = 5 g, Orange = 5 g, Black = 5 g, White = 5 g, Purple = 5 g, Brown = 5 g and a little bit of Red to embroider the mouth
- 3.00 mm hook
- Polyester fiberfill = 40 g
- Tapestry needle
- Twelve 4 mm black beads for eyes or other eyes as desired
- Sewing needle and thread for attaching eyes

These are small dolls. You can use left over yarn to make colorful petals.

Size

Flowers are 4 inches (10 cm) high, sitting position.
Bugs are 3.5 inches (9 cm) high, sitting position.

Note

Flowers and Bugs have same basic patterns; Legs, Arms, Head, Body and Cap.

Head

Rnd 1: With **Cream** or **Brown** (skin color), ch 2, 6 sc in second chain from hook. (6)
Rnd 2: 2 sc in each st around. (12)
Rnd 3: (Sc in next st, 2 sc in next st) around. (18)
Rnd 4: (Sc in next 2 sts, 2 sc in next st) around. (24)
Rnd 5-7: Sc in each st around.
Rnd 8: (Sc in next 2 sts, sc next 2 sts tog) around. (18)
Rnd 9: Sc in each st around.
Rnd 10: (Sc next 2 sts tog, sc in next st) around. Stuff. (12)
Rnd 11: Sc next 2 sts tog around, sl st in first st. Fasten off. Sew opening close. (6)

Cap

Rnd 1: With **Green/ Black** or **Brown**, ch 2, 6 sc in second chain from hook. (6)
Rnd 2: 2 sc in each st around. (12)
Rnd 3: (Sc in next st, 2 sc in next st) around. (18)
Rnd 4: (2 sc in next st, sc in next 2 sts) around. (24)
Rnd 5: (Sc in next 4 sts, 2 sc in next st) 4 times, sc in next 4 sts. (28)
Rnd 6-9: Sc in each st around.
Rnd 10: Sc in each st around, join with sl st in first st. Leave long end for sewing, fasten off.

Put cap over head and sew.

Body

Rnd 1: With **Green/ Black** or **Brown** (body color), ch 2, 6 sc in second chain from hook. (6)
Rnd 2: 2 sc in each st around. (12)
Rnd 3: (Sc in next st, 2 sc in next st) around. (18)
Rnd 4-8: Sc in each st around.
Rnd 9: (Sc next 2 sts tog, sc in next st) around. (12)
Rnd 10: (Sc next 2 sts tog, sc in next st) around, sl st in first st. Leave long end for sewing, fasten off. Stuff. (8)

For Bee: Rnds 4 and Rnd 7 are **Yellow**. Rnds 1-3, Rnds 5-6 and Rnds 8-10 are **Brown**.

For Bee & Ladybug: Sew body to rnds 7-9 of cap.

For Flowers need to sew petals to head before sew body to head.

Leg

Make 2.

Rnd 1: With **Cream** or **Brown** (feet or skin color), ch 2, 5 sc in second chain from hook. (5)

Rnd 2: Sc in each st around, changing to **Green/ Black** or **Brown** (body color) in last 2 loops of last st.

Rnd 3-4: Sc in each st around.

Rnd 5: Sc in each st around, join with sl st in first st. Fasten off.

Arm

Make 2.

Rnd 1: With **Cream** or **Brown** (hand or skin color), ch 2, 5 sc in second chain from hook, changing to **Green/ Black** or **Brown** (body color) in last 2 loops of last st. (5)

Rnd 2-4: Sc in each st around.

Rnd 5: Sc in each st around, join with sl st in first st. Fasten off.

Pink & Purple Flowers

Petal

Make 7 each in pink and purple.

Rnd 1: With **Pink**, ch 2, 6 sc in second chain from hook. (6)

Rnd 2: 2 sc in each st around. (12)

Rnd 3: (Sc in next st, 2 sc in next st) around. (18)

Rnd 4-5: Sc in each st around.

Rnd 6: (Sc next 2 sts tog, sc in next st) around. (12)

Rnd 7: Sc next 2 sts tog around, sl st in first st. Leave long end for sewing, fasten off. (6)

Pin petals on rnds 10 of cap and sew to cap.

Finishing

Sew body to rnds 7-9 of cap. Sew arms to rnd 10 of body. Sew legs to rnd 3 of body.

Sew eyes 5 sts apart. With **Red**, embroider mouth.

Yellow & Orange Flowers

Petals

Make 10 each in yellow and orange.

Rnd 1: With **Orange**, ch 2, 3 sc in second chain from hook. (3)

Rnd 2: 2 sc in each st around. (6)

Rnd 3: Sc in each st around.

Rnd 4: (Sc in next st, 2 sc in next st) around. (9)

Rnd 5: Sc in each st around.

Rnd 6: (Sc next 2 sts tog, sc in next st) around, sl st in first st. Leave long end for sewing, fasten off. (6)

Pin petals on rnds 10 of cap and sew to cap.

Finishing

Sew body to rnds 7-9 of cap. Sew arms to rnd 10 of body. Sew legs to rnd 3 of body.
Sew eyes 5 sts apart. With **Red**, embroider mouth.

Bee

Wing

Make 2.

Rnd 1: With **White**, ch 2, 6 sc in second chain from hook. (6)
Rnd 2: 2 sc in each st around. (12)
Rnd 3: (Sc in next st, 2 sc in next st) around. (18)
Rnd 4-5: Sc in each st around.
Rnd 6: (Sc next 2 sts tog, sc in next st) around. (12)
Rnd 7: Sc next 2 sts tog around, sl st in first st. Leave long end for sewing, fasten off. (6)

Sew rnd 7 of wings together.
Sew wings on middle back of body.

Antenna

Make 2.

Rnd 1: With **Brown**, ch 6, 3 sc in second chain from hook, sc in next 4 chs, fasten off. (7)

Pin antenna 3 sts apart on rnd 8 of cap and sew to cap.

Finishing

Sew arms to rnd 10 of body. Sew legs to rnd 3 of body. Sew eyes 5 sts apart. With **Red**, embroider mouth.

Ladybug

Wing

Make 2.

Rnd 1: With **Red**, ch 2, 6 sc in second chain from hook. (6)
Rnd 2: 2 sc in each st around. (12)
Rnd 3: (Sc in next st, 2 sc in next st) around. (18)

Fold wing in half, matching sts, working in rnd 3 through both thicknesses, sc in next 8 sts. Leave long end for sewing, fasten off. (8)

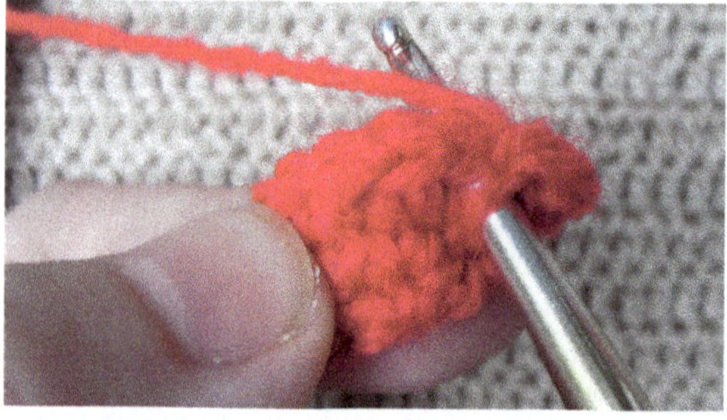

With **Black**, embroider dots on wings.

Sew wings together as in picture below.

Sew wings on middle back of body.

Antenna

Make 2.

Rnd 1: With **Black**, ch 6, 3 sc in second chain from hook, sc in next 4 chs, fasten off. (7)
Pin antenna 3 sts apart on rnd 8 of cap and sew to cap.

Finishing

Sew arms to rnd 10 of body. Sew legs to rnd 3 of body. Sew eyes 5 sts apart. With **Red**, embroider mouth.

Rainbow Flowers

Materials

- No 2 yarn (Sport, Baby) 2 fine
  Catania yarn from Schachenmayr SMC;
  Green = 40 g, Taupe = 45 g, Dark Blue = 5 g,
  Blue = 15 g, Jade = 20 g, Apple Green = 20 g,
  Yellow = 20 g, Orange = 20 g and Red = 20 g
- 4.00 mm hook
- Polyester fiberfill = 100 g (one flower)
- Tapestry needle
- Strong iron wire (16 gauge wire)
  26 inches/ 65 cm long for stem and root,
  Strong iron wire 13 inches/ 32.5 cm long
  for leaf.
- Pliers for cutting and bending the wire
- Pins
- Bucket or Flower Pot. Diameter of the bottom: 3.2-4.2 inches/8-10.5cm, diameter of the top: 5- 5.8 inches/ 12.5-14.5cm, high: 4.6 inches/ 11.5 cm
- All purpose Glue (use to glue root to the flower pot in case Flower does not fit properly)
- 10 mm Safety Eyes for making face of Flower (Optional)

These flowers are crocheted using 2 strands of yarn. Instead of 2 strands you can use Worsted Weight yarn and a 4 mm hook.

Size

Flower diameter is 9.5 inches/ 23.75 cm, 16 inches/ 40 cm high (from bottom of the Root to top of the highest Petal)

Note

Crochet using 2 strands of yarn. If you use Worsted weight yarn, crochet using 1 strand of yarn.

Petal

Make 6, crochet using 2 strands of yarn.

Rnd 1: With 2 strands of **Red**, ch 5, sc in second chain from hook, sc in next 2 chs, 3 sc in last ch; working in remaining loops on opposite side of chain, sc in next 2 chs, 2 sc in next ch. (10)

	x	x	x	x	o
x	o	o	o	o	x
	x	x	x	x	

o = chain x = sc

Rnd 2: 2 sc in next st, sc in next 2 sts, 2 sc in next 3 sts, sc in next 2 sts, 2 sc in next 2 sts. (16)
Rnd 3: 2 sc in next st, sc in next 3 sts, (2 sc in next st, sc in next st) 3 times, sc in next 2 sts, (2 sc in next st, sc in next st) 2 times. (22)
Rnd 4: Sc in next 2 sts, 2 sc in next st, sc in next 4 sts, (2 sc in next st, sc in next 2 sts) 2 times, 2 sc in next st, sc in next 4 sts, 2 sc in next st, sc in next 2 sts, 2 sc in next st, changing to **Dark orange** in last two loops of last st. (28)
Rnd 5-6: Sc in each st around. (28)
Rnd 7: Sc in each st around, changing to **Yellow** in last two loops of last st. (28)
Rnd 8-9: Sc in each st around. (28)
Rnd 10: (Sc next 2 sts tog, sc in next 12 sts) 2 times, changing to **Apple green** in last two loops of last st. (26)
Rnd 11: Sc in each st around. (26)
Rnd 12: (Sc next 2 sts tog, sc in next 11 sts) 2 times. (24)
Rnd 13: Sc in each st around, changing to **Jade** in last two loops of last st. (24)
Rnd 14: (Sc next 2 sts tog, sc in next 10 sts) 2 times. (22)
Rnd 15: Sc in each st around. (22)
Rnd 16: (Sc next 2 sts tog, sc in next 9 sts) 2 times, changing to **Blue** in last two loops of last st. (20)
Rnd 17: Sc in each st around. (20)
Rnd 18: (Sc next 2 sts tog, sc in next 8 sts) 2 times. (18)
Rnd 19: Sc in each st around, join with sl st in first st, fasten off. (18)

Sew 6 Petals together on Rnd 17-19 (Blue color) to make a circle.

Sew the opening of Petals close after you finish sewing the 6 petals together.

Middle of Flower, Stem and Root

Crochet using 2 strands of yarn. Start from middle top of Flower to bottom of Root.

Rnd 1: With 2 strands of **Yellow**, ch 2, 6 sc in second chain from hook. (6)

Rnd 2: 2 sc in each st around, changing to **Apple green** in last two loops of last st. (12)

Rnd 3: (Sc in next st, 2 sc in next st) around. (18)

Rnd 4: (2 sc in next st, sc in next 2 sts) around, changing to **Jade** in last two loops of last st. (24)

Rnd 5: (Sc in next 3 sts, 2 sc in next st) around. (30)

Rnd 6: Sc in next 2 sts, 2 sc in next st, (sc in next 4 sts, 2 sc in next st) 5 times, sc in next 2 sts, changing to **Blue** in last two loops of last st. (36)

Rnd 7: (Sc in next 5 sts, 2 sc in next st) around, changing to **Dark blue** in last two loops of last st. (42)

Rnd 8: Sc in next 3 sts, 2 sc in next st, (sc in next 6 sts, 2 sc in next st) 5 times, sc in next 3 sts. (48)

Rnd 9: Sc in each st around, changing to **Green** (color of back of the flower & stem) in last two loops of last st. (48)

Rnd 10: <u>Working in back loops only</u>. (Sc in next 6 sts, sc next 2 sts tog) around. (42)

Rnd 11: (Sc in next 5 sts, sc next 2 sts tog) around. (36)

Rnd 12: (Sc in next 4 sts, sc next 2 sts tog) around. (30)

Rnd 13: (Sc in next 3 sts, sc next 2 sts tog) around. (24)

Rnd 14: (Sc in next 2 sts, sc next 2 sts tog) around. (18)

Optional: Making face for Flower.

Insert safety eyes 5-6 sts apart between rnds 5-6. With **Red** yarn embroider mouth. Stuff.

Rnd 15: (Sc in next st, sc next 2 sts tog) around. Stuff. (12)

Rnd 16: (Sc in next 2 sts, sc next 2 sts tog) around. (9)

Rnd 17-55: Sc in each st around. (9)

Rnd 56: Sc in each st around, changing to **Taupe** (color of root) in last two loops of last st. (9)
Rnd 57: 2 sc in each st around. (18)
Rnd 58: (Sc in next st, 2 sc in next st) around. (27)
Rnd 59: (2 sc in next st, sc in next 2 sts) around. (36)
Rnd 60: (Sc in next 3 sts, 2 sc in next st) around. (45)
Rnd 61: Sc in next 2 sts, (2 sc in next st, sc in next 4 sts) 8 times, 2 sc in next st, sc in next 2 sts. (54)
Rnd 62-63: Sc in each st around. (54)
Rnd 64: Sc in next 4 sts, (2 sc in next st, sc in next 8 sts) 5 times, 2 sc in next st, sc in next 4 sts. (60)
Rnd 65-72: Sc in each st around. (60)
Rnd 73: (Sc next 2 sts tog, sc in next 8 sts) around. (54)
Rnd 74: (Sc next 2 sts tog, sc in next 7 sts) around. (48)
Rnd 75: (Sc next 2 sts tog, sc in next 6 sts) around. (42)
Rnd 76: (Sc next 2 sts tog, sc in next 5 sts) around. (36)
Rnd 77: (Sc next 2 sts tog, sc in next 4 sts) around. (30)
Rnd 78: (Sc next 2 sts tog, sc in next 3 sts) around. (24)
Rnd 79: (Sc next 2 sts tog, sc in next 2 sts) around. Do not fasten off or cut the yarn. (18)

Insert iron wire and stuff Root.
Do not stuff Stem.

Fold 26 inch Iron wire in half twist the wire up together and fold them at the end.

Insert iron wire through the Root and go up to back of Flower. (All the way to the top. See the black line in the picture below.)

Stuff the Root tightly and try to keep the iron wire in the middle otherwise the Flower might not stand up straight.

Continue to make Rnds 80-81.

Rnd 80: (Sc next 2 sts tog, sc in next st) around. (12)

Rnd 81: Sc next 2 sts tog around, join with sl st in first st, fasten off. Sew the opening close. (6)

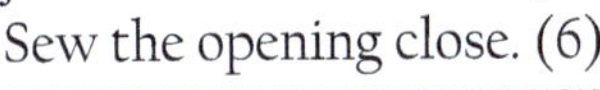

Leaf

Crochet using 2 strands of yarn.

Rnd 1: With 2 strands of **Green** (leaf color), ch 2, 6 sc in second chain from hook. (6)

Rnd 2: (Sc in next st, 2 sc in next st) around. (9)

Rnd 3: (Sc in next 2 sts, 2 sc in next st) around. (12)

Rnd 4: (Sc in next 3 sts, 2 sc in next st) around. (15)

Rnd 5: Sc in next 2 sts, 2 sc in next st, (sc in next 4 sts, 2 sc in next st) 2 times, sc in next 2 sts. (18)

Rnd 6: (Sc in next 5 sts, 2 sc in next st) around. (21)

Rnd 7: Sc in next 3 sts, 2 sc in next st, (sc in next 6 sts, 2 sc in next st) 2 times, sc in next 3 sts. (24)

Rnd 8: Sc in each st around. (24)

Rnd 9: (Sc in next 7 sts, 2 sc in next st) around. (27)

Rnd 10-20: Sc in each st around. (27)

Rnd 21: (Sc next 2 sts tog, sc in next 7 sts) around. (24)

Rnd 22: Sc in each st around. (24)

Rnd 23: Sc in next 3 sts, sc next 2 sts tog, (sc in next 6 sts, sc next 2 sts tog) 2 times, sc in next 3 sts. (21)

Rnd 24: Sc in each st around. (21)

Rnd 25: (Sc next 2 sts tog, sc in next 5 sts) around. (18)

Rnd 26: Sc in each st around. (18)

Rnd 27: Sc in next 2 sts, sc next 2 sts tog, (sc in next 4 sts, sc next 2 sts tog) 2 times, sc in next 2 sts. (15)

Rnd 28: Sc in each st around. (15)

Rnd 29: (Sc next 2 sts tog, sc in next 3 sts) around. Do not fasten off or cut the yarn. (12)

Insert iron wire. Do not stuff Leaf.

Fold 13 inch Iron wire in half twist the wire up together and fold them at the end.

Insert iron wire through inside the Leaf.

Continue to make Rnds 30-36.

Rnd 30: Sc in each st around. (12)

Rnd 31: (Sc next 2 sts tog, sc in next 2 sts) around. (9)

Rnd 32-35: Sc in each st around. (9)

Row 36: Working in row, flatten last rnd, matching sts and working through both thicknesses, sc in next 3 sts, sl st in next st. Leave long end for sewing, fasten off.

Finishing

Pin Petals behind the Flower. Sew the last round of petals to the middle of Flower on rnd 10 (under free loops of rnd 9).

Pin Leaf on one side of Stem, sew Rnds 33-36 of Leaf to Rnds 53-56 of Stem.

Put Flower in a Pot or Bucket. If it does not fit properly, use glue or double sided tape to stick it to the pot.

Sunflower

Materials

- No 2 yarn (Sport, Baby) 2 fine
  Catania yarn from Schachenmayr SMC;
  Green = 80 g, Dark brown = 40 g,
  Yellow = 45 g and Taupe = 45 g
- 4.00 mm hook
- Polyester fiberfill = 135 g
- Tapestry needle
- Strong iron wire (16 gauge wire)
  29 inches/ 73.5 cm long for stem and root,
  Strong iron wire 13 inches/ 32.5 cm long for leaf.
- Pins
- Bucket or Flower Pot. Diameter of the bottom: 3.2-4.2 inches/8-10.5cm, diameter of the top: 5- 5.8 inches/ 12.5-14.5cm, high: 4.6 inches/ 11.5 cm
- All purpose Glue (used to glue the root to the flower pot in case Flower does not fit properly)
- 15 mm Safety Eyes for making face of Flower (Optional)
- Pliers for cutting and bending the wire

You can use Worsted weight yarn and 4 mm hook as well.

Size

Flower diameter is 9.5 inches/ 23.75 cm, height: 16 inches/ 40 cm (from bottom of the Root to top of the highest Petal).

Note

Crochet using 2 strands of yarn. If you use Worsted weight yarn, crochet using 1 strand of yarn.

Middle of Flower, Stem and Root

Crochet using 2 strands of yarn. Starting from middle top of Flower to bottom of Root.

Rnd 1: With 2 strands of **Brown**, ch 2, 6 sc in second chain from hook. (6)
Rnd 2: 2 sc in each st around. (12)
Rnd 3: (Sc in next st, 2 sc in next st) around. (18)
Rnd 4: (2 sc in next st, sc in next 2 sts) around. (24)
Rnd 5: (Sc in next 3 sts, 2 sc in next st) around. (30)
Rnd 6: Sc in next 2 sts, 2 sc in next st, (sc in next 4 sts, 2 sc in next st) 5 times, sc in next 2 sts. (36)
Rnd 7: (Sc in next 5 sts, 2 sc in next st) around. (42)
Rnd 8: Sc in next 3 sts, 2 sc in next st, (sc in next 6 sts, 2 sc in next st) 5 times, sc in next 3 sts. (48)
Rnd 9: (Sc in next 7 sts, 2 sc in next st) around. (54)
Rnd 10: Sc in next 4 sts, 2 sc in next st, (sc in next 8 sts, 2 sc in next st) 5 times, sc in next 4 sts. (60)
Rnd 11: (Sc in next 9 sts, 2 sc in next st) around. (66)
Rnd 12: Sc in next 5 sts, 2 sc in next st, (sc in next 10 sts, 2 sc in next st) 5 times, sc in next 5 sts. (72)
Rnd 13: (Sc in next 11 sts, 2 sc in next st) around. (78)
Rnd 14: Sc in next 6 sts, 2 sc in next st, (sc in next 12 sts, 2 sc in next st) 5 times, sc in next 6 sts. (84)
Rnd 15: (Sc in next 13 sts, 2 sc in next st) around. (90)
Rnd 16: Sc in next 7 sts, 2 sc in next st, (sc in next 14 sts, 2 sc in next st) 5 times, sc in next 7 sts, changing to **Green** (color of back of the flower & stem) in last two loops of last st. (96)
Rnd 17: <u>Working in back loops only.</u> (Sc in next 14 sts, sc next 2 sts tog) around. (90)
Rnd 18: (Sc next 2 sts tog, sc in next 13 sts) around. (84)
Rnd 19: Sc in next 6 sts, sc next 2 sts tog, (sc in next 12 sts, sc next 2 sts tog) 5 times, sc in next 6 sts. (78)
Rnd 20: (Sc in next 11 sts, sc next 2 sts tog) around. (72)
Rnd 21: Sc in next 5 sts, sc next 2 sts tog, (sc in next 10 sts, sc next 2 sts tog) 5 times, sc in next 5 sts. (66)
Rnd 22: (Sc in next 9 sts, sc next 2 sts tog) around. (60)
Rnd 23: Sc in next 4 sts, sc next 2 sts tog, (sc in next 8 sts, sc next 2 sts tog) 5 times, sc in next 4 sts. (54)
Rnd 24: (Sc in next 7 sts, sc next 2 sts tog) around. (48)
Rnd 25: Sc in next 3 sts, sc next 2 sts tog, (sc in next 6 sts, sc next 2 sts tog) 5 times, sc in next 3 sts. (42)
Rnd 26: (Sc in next 5 sts, sc next 2 sts tog) around. (36)

Optional: Making face for Flower.

Insert safety eyes 10 sts apart between rnds 7-8. Stuff. With **Red** yarn embroider mouth.

Rnd 27: Sc in next 2 sts, sc next 2 sts tog, (sc in next 4 sts, sc next 2 sts tog) 5 times, sc in next 2 sts. (30)
Rnd 28: (Sc in next 3 sts, sc next 2 sts tog) around. (24)
Rnd 29: Sc in next st, sc next 2sts tog, (sc in next 2 sts, sc next 2 sts tog) 5 times, sc in next st. (18)
Rnd 30: (Sc in next st, sc next 2 sts tog) around. Stuff. (12)
Rnd 31: (Sc in next 2 sts, sc next 2 sts tog) around. (9)
Rnd 32-73: Sc in each st around. (9)

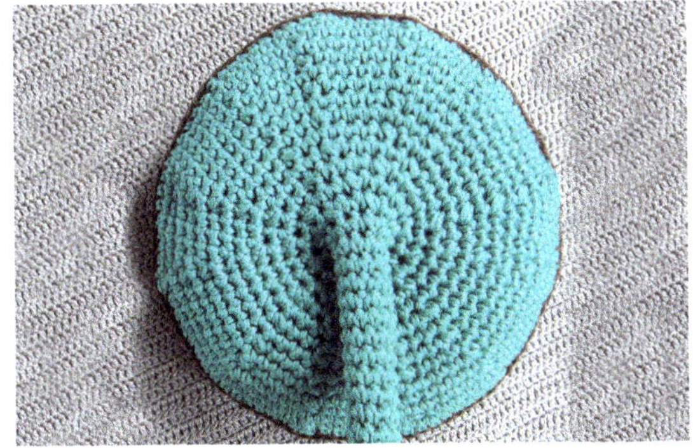

Rnd 74: Sc in each st around, changing to **Taupe** (color of root) in last two loops of last st. (9)
Rnd 75: 2 sc in each st around. (18)
Rnd 76: (Sc in next st, 2 sc in next st) around. (27)
Rnd 77: (2 sc in next st, sc in next 2 sts) around. (36)
Rnd 78: (Sc in next 3 sts, 2 sc in next st) around. (45)
Rnd 79: Sc in next 2 sts, (2 sc in next st, sc in next 4 sts) 8 times, 2 sc in next st, sc in next 2 sts. (54)
Rnd 80-81: Sc in each st around. (54)
Rnd 82: Sc in next 4 sts, (2 sc in next st, sc in next 8 sts) 5 times, 2 sc in next st, sc in next 4 sts. (60)
Rnd 83-90: Sc in each st around. (60)
Rnd 91: (Sc next 2 sts tog, sc in next 8 sts) around. (54)
Rnd 92: (Sc next 2 sts tog, sc in next 7 sts) around. (48)
Rnd 93: (Sc next 2 sts tog, sc in next 6 sts) around. (42)
Rnd 94: (Sc next 2 sts tog, sc in next 5 sts) around. (36)
Rnd 95: (Sc next 2 sts tog, sc in next 4 sts) around. (30)
Rnd 96: (Sc next 2 sts tog, sc in next 3 sts) around. (24)
Rnd 97: (Sc next 2 sts tog, sc in next 2 sts) around. (18)
Do not fasten off or cut the yarn.

Insert iron wire and stuff Root. Do not stuff Stem.

Fold 29 inch Iron wire in half, twist the wire up together and fold them at the end.
Insert iron wire through the Root and go up to back of Flower. (See pictures on page 24.)
Stuff the Root tightly and try to keep the iron wire in the middle, otherwise the Flower might not stand up straight.

Continue to make Rnds 98-99.

Rnd 98: (Sc next 2 sts tog, sc in next st) around. (12)
Rnd 99: Sc next 2 sts tog around, join with sl st in first st, fasten off. Sew the opening close. (6)

Circle of Petals

Make 2.

With 2 strands of **Yellow**, (ch 10, sl st in second chain from hook, sc in next ch, hdc in next ch, dc in next 6 chs) 26 times, fasten off.

Tie both ends together to make a circle.
The picture shows the wrong side up (the petals curl in).

Put the 2 Circles together: the bottom Circle with the wrong side up. (The two Circles are facing each other.) The petals of top Circle stay between the petals of bottom Circle (see pictures below).

Top circle

Bottom circle

Crochet 2 Circles together by using single crochet stitches. With 2 strands of **Yellow** yarn, sc around, leave long end for sewing, fasten off (see pictures below: x = sc). (total stitches = 52)

Leaf Rnds 1-32 same as Rainbow Flower's leaf (see page 25)

Row 33: <u>Working in row</u>, flatten last rnd, matching sts and working through both thicknesses, sc in next 3 sts, sl st in next st. Leave long end for sewing, fasten off.

Finishing

Pin Petals behind the Flower. Sew the last round of petals to the middle of Flower on rnd 17.

Pin Leaf on one side of Stem, sew Rnds 26-33 of Leaf to Rnds 67-74 of Stem.

Put Flower in a Pot or Bucket. If it does not fit properly, use glue or double sided tape to stick it to the pot.

Four Seasons Birds

Material

- No 2 yarn (Sport, Baby)
  Catania yarn from Schachenmayr SMC;
  Birds: Green = 15 g, White = 15 g,
  Orange = 15 g, Blue = 15 g
- Eggs: Blue = 5 g, Pink = 5 g, Yellow = 5 g,
  Green = 5 g or you can use any color.
- Flowers: Blue = 5 g, Pink = 5 g, Yellow = 5 g,
  Green = 5 g, Brown = 5 g or you can use any color
- Candy Corn: White = 5 g, Yellow = 5 g,
  Orange = 5 g
- Christmas Tree: Green = 15 g
- Christmas Hat: Red = 5 g, Green = 5 g
- 3.00 mm hook
- Red embroidery floss
- 10 mm Bells
- Polyester fiberfill = 50 g
- Black 5 mm beads for eyes or other eyes as desired
- Tapestry needle
- Sewing needle and thread for attaching eyes
- Brown Chenilles Stems
  (a.k.a. Pipe Cleaners) for flower stems
- Tiny Flower Pots, Foam and Glue

Size

Bird is 2 inches tall (10 cm).
Egg is 1 inch tall (2.5 cm).
Flower diameter is 2.2 inches (5.5 cm).
Candy Corn is 1 inch tall (2.5 cm).
Christmas Tree is 3 inches tall (7.5 cm).

Bird

Body

Crochet from top to bottom of the body.

Rnd 1: With **Green** (body color) , ch 6, sc in second chain from hook, sc in next 3 chs, 3 sc in next ch; working in remaining loops on opposite side of chain, sc in next 3 chs, 2 sc in next ch. (12)

	x	x	x	x	x	o
x	o	o	o	o	o	x
	x	x	x	x	x	

o = chain x = sc

Rnd 2: 2 sc in next st, sc in next 3 sts, 2 sc in next 3 sts, sc in next 3 sts, 2 sc in next 2 sts. (18)

Rnd 3: 2 sc in next st, sc in next 4 sts, (2 sc in next st, sc in next st) 3 times, sc in next 3 sts, (2 sc in next st, sc in next st) 2 times. (24)

Rnd 4: 2 sc in next st, sc in next 5 sts, (2 sc in next st, sc in next 2 sts) 3 times, sc in next 3 sts, (2 sc in next st, sc in next 2 sts) 2 times. (30)

Rnd 5: Sc in each st around.

Rnd 6: (2 sc in next st, sc in next 4 sts) around. (36)

Rnd 7: Sc in each st around.

Rnd 8: (Sc in next 5 sts, 2 sc in next st) around. (42)

Rnd 9-15: Sc in each st around.

Rnd 16: (Sc next 2 sts tog, sc in next 5 sts) around. (36)

Rnd 17: Sc in next 2 sts, sc next 2 sts tog, (sc in next 4 sts, sc next 2 sts tog) 5 times, sc in next 2 sts. (30)

Rnd 18: (Sc in in next 3 sts, sc next 2 sts tog) around. (24)

Rnd 19: Sc in next st, sc next 2 sts tog, (sc in next 2 sts, sc next 2 sts tog) 5 times, sc in next st. Stuff. (18)

Rnd 20: (Sc in next st, sc next 2 sts tog) around. (12)

Rnd 21: Sc next 2 sts tog around, join with sl st in first st, fasten off. (6)

Wing

Make 2, do not stuff.

Rnd 1: With **Green** (wing color), ch 2, 6 sc in second chain from hook. (6)

Rnd 2: (2 sc in next st, sc in next st) around. (9)

Rnd 3: Sc in each st around. (9)

Rnd 4: (Sc in next 2 sts, 2 sc in next st) around. (12)

Rnd 5: Sc in each st around.

Rnd 6: (Sc in next 3 sts, 2 sc in next st) around. (15)

Rnd 7: (Sc in next st, sc next 2 sts tog) around. (10)

Rnd 8: (Sc in next 3 sts, sc next 2 sts tog) around, join with sl st in first st. Leave long end for sewing, fasten off. (8)

Do not stuff wings, sew to body on rnd 9.

Tail

Do not stuff.

Rnd 1: With **Green** (tail color). Ch 6, sc in second chain from hook, sc in next 3 chs, 3 sc in next ch; working in remaining loops on opposite side of chain, sc in next 3 chs, 2 sc in next ch. (12)

	x	x	x	x	x	o
x	o	o	o	o	o	x
	x	x	x	x	x	

o = chain x = sc

Rnd 2: 2 sc in next st, sc in next 3 sts, 2 sc in next 3 sts, sc in next 3 sts, 2 sc in next 2 sts. (18)
Rnd 3-5: Sc in next st around.
Rnd 6: (Sc in next 4 sts, sc next 2 sts tog) around. (15)
Rnd 7: Sc in each st around.
Rnd 8: (Sc next 2 sts tog, sc in next 3 sts) around. (12)
Rnd 9: Sc in each st around.
Rnd 10: (Sc in next 2 sts, sc next 2 sts tog) around. (9)
Rnd 11: Sc in each st around.
Rnd 12: Sc in each st around, join with sl st in first st. Leave long end for sewing, fasten off. Sew tail to body on rnds 18-20.

Finishing

Sew eyes 8 sts apart between rnds 7-8 of head. With **Red** embroidery floss, embroider mouth over rnds 8-9 (see pictures below).

Eggs

Rnd 1: With **Blue** (egg color), ch 2,
6 sc in second chain from hook. (6)
Rnd 2: 2 sc in each st around. (12)
Rnd 3: (Sc in next 3 sts, 2 sc in next st) around. (15)
Rnd 4-5: Sc in each st around.
Rnd 6: (Sc in next 3 sts, sc next 2 sts tog) around. (12)
Rnd 7: Sc in each st around. Stuff.
Rnd 8: Sc next 2 sts tog around, join with sl st in first st, fasten off. (6)

Flowers

Middle of flower
Rnd 1: With **Yellow** (color of the middle of flower), ch 2, 6 sc in second chain from hook. (6)
Rnd 2: 2 sc in each st around. (12)
Rnd 3: (Sc in next st, 2 sc in next st) around. (18)
Rnd 4: (Sc in next 2 sts, 2 sc in next st) around. (24)
Rnd 5: Working in back loops only. (Sc next 2 sts tog, sc in next 2 sts) around. (18)
Rnd 6: (Sc next 2 sts tog, sc in next st) around. (12)
Rnd 7: Sc next 2 sts tog around, join with sl st in first st, fasten off. (6)

Petals Join **Dark pink** to free loop of rnd 4, ch 1, sc in same st, (ch 4, sl st in second ch from hook, ch 2, sc in next st) around, fasten off.
Put the Brown Chenilles Stem (Pipe Cleaner) through middle of the back of flower, then fold it and twist together.

Cut foam in a small cubic shape and put it in the flower pot.
Glue green or brown yarn on top of foam.
Stick flower in the middle of the pot.

Candy Corn

Rnd 1: With **Yellow**, ch 6, sc in second chain from hook, sc in next 3 chs, 3 sc in next ch; working in remaining loops on opposite side of chain, sc in next 3 chs, 2 sc in next ch. (12)

	x	x	x	x	x	o
x	o	o	o	o	o	x
	x	x	x	x	x	

o = chain x = sc

Rnd 2: Sc in each st around.
Rnd 3: Sc in each st around, changing to **Orange** in last 2 loops of last st.
Rnd 4: (Sc next 2 sts tog, sc in next 2 sts) around. (9)
Rnd 5: Sc in each st around, changing to **White** in last 2 loops of last st. Stuff.
Rnd 6: (Sc next 2 sts tog, sc in next st) around. (6)
Rnd 7: Sc in each st around, join with sl st in first st, fasten off. (6)

Christmas Hat

Rnd 1: With **Red** (hat color), ch 2, 6 sc in second chain from hook. (6)
Rnd 2: Sc in each st around.
Rnd 3: (Sc in next st, 2 sc in next st) around. (9)
Rnd 4: (Sc in next 2 sts, 2 sc in next st) around. (12)
Rnd 5: (Sc in next 3 sts, 2 sc in next st) around, changing to **Green** in last 2 loops of last st. (15)
Rnd 6: Sc in each st around, sl st in first st. Leave long end for sewing, fasten off.

Sew bell on top of the hat, sew hat to one side of the head.

Christmas Tree

Rnd 1: With **Green** (tree color), ch 2, 6 sc in second chain from hook. (6)
Rnd 2: Sc in each st around.
Rnd 3: (Sc in next st, 2 sc in next st) around. (9)
Rnd 4: Sc in each st around.
Rnd 5: (Sc in next 2 sts, 2 sc in next st) around. (12)
Rnd 6: (Sc in next 3 sts, 2 sc in next st) around. (15)
Rnd 7: (Sc in next 4 sts, 2 sc in next st) around. (18)
Rnd 8: (Sc in next 5 sts, 2 sc in next st) around. (21)
Rnd 9: (Sc in next 6 sts, 2 sc in next st) around. (24)
Rnd 10: (Sc in next 7 sts, 2 sc in next st) around. (27)
Rnd 11: (Sc in next 8 sts, 2 sc in next st) around. (30)
Rnd 12: (Sc in next 9 sts, 2 sc in next st) around. (33)
Rnd 13: Sc in next 5 sts, 2 sc in next st, (sc in next 10 sts, 2 sc in next st) 2 times, sc in next 5 sts. (36)
Rnd 14: (Sc in next 11 sts, 2 sc in next st) around. (39)
Rnd 15: Sc in next 6 sts, 2 sc in next st, (sc in next 12 sts, 2 sc in next st) 2 times, sc in next 6 sts, join with sl st in first st, fasten off. (42)

Sew bells on top of the tree and around it as shown in picture above.

Easter Bears

Materials

- No 2 yarn (Sport, Baby)
  4 ply Acrylic yarn; Brown = 20 g, Light pink = 30 g, White = 20 g, Cream = 5 g, Red = 20 g
- 3.25 mm hook (US: D, UK: 10)
- 4 mm hook (US: G, UK: 8) for making Basket
- Polyester fiberfill = 20 g

- 4 Black 8 mm buttons for eyes or other eyes as desired
- Tapestry needle
- Sewing needle and thread for attaching eyes
- Black embroidery floss
- Pins

Size

Sitting bear is 3 inches (7.5 cm) tall.
Standing bear is 4.5 inches tall (11.5 cm).
These sizes exclude the hats.
Basket diameter: 3 inches (7.5 cm), height: 2.5 inches (6.5 cm).

Notes

The bears have same basic patterns for Legs, Arms, Head & Body, Ears, Muzzle and Cap.

Head and Body

Work from top of the head to bottom of the body.

Rnd 1: With **Brown**, ch 2, 6 sc in second chain from hook. (6 sc made)
Rnd 2: 2 sc in each st around. (12)
Rnd 3: (Sc in next st, 2 sc in next st) around. (18)
Rnd 4: (2 sc in next st, sc in next 2 sts) around. (24)
Rnd 5: Sc in next 2 sts, 2 sc in next st, (sc in next 3 sts, 2 sc in next st) 5 times, sc in next st. (30)
Rnd 6: (Sc in next 4 sts, 2 sc next st) around. (36)
Rnd 7-12: Sc in each st around.
Rnd 13: (Sc next 2 sts tog, sc in next 4 sts) around. (30)
Rnd 14: (Sc next 2 sts tog, sc in next 3 sts) around. (24)
Rnd 15: (Sc next 2 sts tog, sc in next 2 sts) around. (18)
Rnd 16: (Sc next 2 sts tog, sc in next st) around, changing to **Light pink** or **white** (body color) in last 2 loops of last st. (12)
Rnd 17: (2 sc in next st, sc in next st) around. Stuff head. (18)
Rnd 18: (Sc in next 2 sts, 2 sc in next st) around. (24)
Rnd 19-25: Sc in each st around.
Rnd 26: (Sc in next 2 sts, sc next 2 sts tog) around. (18)
Rnd 27: (Sc in next st, sc next 2 sts tog) around. Stuff. (12)
Rnd 28: Sc next 2 sts tog around, join with sl st in first st, fasten off. (6)

Arm

Make 2 for each bear. Only stuff hand.

Rnd 1: With **Brown**, ch 2, 6 sc in second chain from hook. (6)
Rnd 2: (Sc in next st, 2 sc in next st) around. (9)
Rnd 3: Sc in each st around.
Rnd 4: (Sc in next st, sc next 2 sts tog) around. Stuff. (6)
Rnd 5-6: Sc in each st around.
Rnd 7: Sc in each st around, join with sl st in first st. Leave long end for sewing, fasten off. Sew arms to body on rnd 17.

Leg

Make 2 for each bear.

Rnd 1: With **Brown**, ch 3, sc in second chain from hook, 3 sc in next ch; working in remaining loops on opposite side of chain, 2 sc in next ch. (6)

	x	x	o
x	o	o	x
	x	x	

o = chain x = sc

Rnd 2: 2 sc in each st around. (12)
Rnd 3: (Sc in next 2 sts, 2 sc in next st) around. (16)
Rnd 4: (Sc next 2 sts tog, sc in next 2 sts) around. (12)
Rnd 5: (Sc in next 2 sts, sc next 2 sts tog) around. (9)
Rnd 6: Sc in each st around, join with sl st in first st. Leave long end for sewing, fasten off. (9) Stuff legs.

Sitting position: use pins to position legs, sew legs to body.

Standing position: use pins to position legs, sew legs to body.

Ear

Make 2 for each bear.

Rnd 1: With **Brown**, ch 2, 6 sc in second chain from hook. (6)
Rnd 2: 2 sc in each st around. (12)
Rnd 3: Sc in each st around.
Rnd 4: Sc in each st around, join with sl st in first st. Leave long end for sewing, fasten off.
Sew the opening close.

Pin ears on rnds 4 – 8 of head, sew to head.

Bear Muzzle

Make one for each bear.

Rnd 1: With **Cream**, ch 2, 6 sc in second chain from hook. (6)
Rnd 2: (Sc in next st, 2 sc in next st) around, join with sl st in first st. Leave long end for sewing, fasten off. (9)

With **Black** embroidery floss, embroider nose and mouth as in picture.

Sew muzzle on rnds 10 – 13 of head.
Sew eyes 6 sts apart between rnds 9-10 of head.

Cap

Make one each; light pink and white.

Rnd 1: With **Light pink**, ch 2, 6 sc in second chain from hook. (6)
Rnd 2: 2 sc in each st around. (12)
Rnd 3: (Sc in next st, 2 sc in next st) around. (18)
Rnd 4: (2 sc in next st, sc in next 2 sts) around. (24)
Rnd 5: (Sc in next 3 sts, 2 sc in next st) around. (30)
Rnd 6: Sc in next st, 2sc in next st, (sc in next 4 sts, 2sc in next st) 5 times, sc in next 3 sts.(36)
Rnd 7: (Sc in next 5 sts, 2 sc in next st) around. (42)
Rnd 8: Sc in next 3 sts, 2sc in next st, (sc in next 6 sts, 2sc in next st) 5 times, sc in next 3 sts. (48)

Rnd 9-13: Sc in each st around.
Rnd 14: Sc in each st around, join with sl st in first st. Fasten off.

Rooster Cap

Rooster Comb

Working in rows.

Row 1: With **Red**, ch 5, sc in second chain from hook, sc in next 3 chains, turn. (4)
Row 2: First point: Ch 6, dc in third chain from hook, hdc in next 2 chs, sc in next ch, sl st in first st on row 1, Second point: Ch 5, dc in third chain from hook, hdc in next ch, sc in next ch, sl st in next st on row 1, Third point: Ch 4, hdc in third ch from hook, sc in next ch, sl st in next st on row 1, Fourth point: Ch 4, hdc in third ch from hook, sc in next ch, sl st in next st on row 1, leave long end for sewing, fasten off.

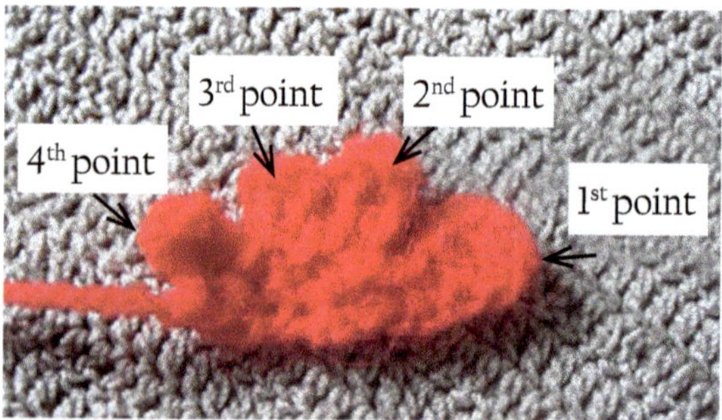

Rooster Tail

Working in rows.

Row 1: With **White**, ch 5, sc in second chain from hook, sc in next 3 chains, turn. (4)
Row 2: First point: Ch 6, dc in third chain from hook, hdc in next 2 chs, sc in next ch, sl st in first st on row 1, Second point: Ch 6, dc in third chain from hook, hdc in next 2 chs, sc in next ch, sl st in next st on row 1,
Third - Fourth points: do the same as Second point, leave long end for sewing, fasten off.

Fold tail in half, sew it together on row 1.

Finishing Rooster Cap and Tail

Sew comb on middle top of cap on rnds 1-2. Sew tail on bottom back of body (rnds 24-25).

Rabbit Cap

Rabbit Ear

Make 2.

Rnd 1: With **Light pink**, ch 2, 6 sc in second chain from hook. (6)

Rnd 2: 2 sc in each st around. (12)

Rnd 3-5: Sc in each st around.

Rnd 6: (Sc next 2 sts tog, sc in next st) around. (8)

Rnd 7-8: Sc in each st around.

Rnd 9: Sc in each st around, join with sl st in first st. Leave long end for sewing, fasten off.

Rabbit Tail

Rnd 1: With **Light pink**, ch 2, 6 sc in second chain from hook. (6)

Rnd 2: Sc in each st around, join with sl st in first st. Leave long end for sewing, fasten off.

Finishing Rabbit Cap and Tail

Sew ears on rnds 3-5 of cap. Sew tail on bottom back of body (rnds 25-26).

Basket

Basket

Use 2 strands of yarn and 4 mm hook (US: G, UK: 8)

Rnd 1: With **Light pink**, ch 2, 6 sc in second chain from hook. (6)
Rnd 2: 2 sc in each st around. (12)
Rnd 3: (Sc in next st, 2 sc in next st) around. (18)
Rnd 4: (2 sc in next st, sc in next 2 sts) around. (24)
Rnd 5: (Sc in next 3 sts, 2 sc in next st) around. (30)
Rnd 6: Sc in next st, 2sc in next st, (sc in next 4 sts, 2sc in next st) 5 times, sc in next 3 sts.(36)
Rnd 7: (Sc in next 5 sts, 2 sc in next st) around. (42)
Rnd 8: Working in back loops only. Sc in each around.
Rnd 9-19: Sc in each st around.
Rnd 20: Sc in next 18 sts, ch 6, skip 3 sts, sc in next 18 sts, ch 6, skip 3 sts, join with sl st in first st. Fasten off.

Red & White Basket

Rnds 1-10: Red color
Rnds 11-13: White color
Rnds 14-16: Red color
Rnds 17-19: White color
Rnds 20: Red color

Sweet Fairy Dolls

Materials

- No 2 yarn (Sport, Baby) 2 fine
  Catania yarn from Schachenmayr SMC; Cream = 30 g, Brown = 20 g, Red = 10 g, Light purple = 10 g, Yellow = 10 g, Orange = 10 g, Pink = 10 g, Green = 10 g, Blue = 10 g, White = 10 g and Dark pink = 10 g
- 3.00 mm hook
- Red embroidery floss
- Polyester fiberfill = 50 g
- Eighteen 5 mm black beads for eyes or other eyes as desired
- Tapestry needle
- Sewing needle and thread for attaching eyes
- Pins

Size

The Fairies are 2.5 inches/ 6.3 cm high.

Note

The Fairies have the same basic patterns for Legs, Arms Head, Body and Wings.

Fairies	Skin color	Dress color	Wings color
Red	cream	red	yellow
White	brown	white	light purple
Blue	brown	blue	dark pink
Yellow	cream	yellow	red
Orange	brown	orange	white
Green	cream	green	pink
Light Purple	cream	light purple	orange
Pink	cream	pink	green
Dark Pink	cream	dark pink	blue

Leg

Make 2 for each Fairy.

Rnd 1: With **Cream** (skin color), ch 2, 6 sc in second chain from hook. (6)

Rnd 2: (Sc in next st, 2 sc in next st) around. (9)

Rnd 3: Sc in each st around. (9)

Rnd 4: Sc in each st around, join with sl st in first st. Fasten off. (9)

Body

Rnd 1: With **Green** (dress color), hold legs together, insert hook in the last round of first leg, pull out the loop from second leg, sc in same st (do not count this st, just for connecting legs together), sc in next 8 sts on second leg (mark first st), sc in next 8 sts on first leg. (16)

The sc is for connecting legs together and go through both legs. The next sc only go through second leg then go round.

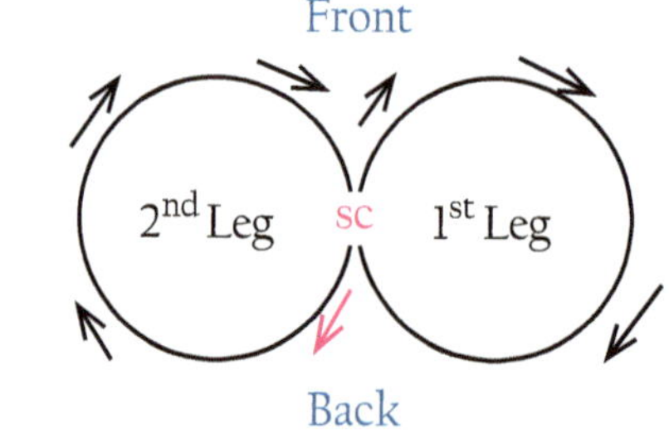

Rnd 2: Sc in next 3 sts, 2 sc in next st, sc in next 7 sts, 2 sc in next st, sc in next 4 sts. (18)

Rnd 3: <u>Working in back loops only.</u>
Sc in each st around. (18)

Rnd 4: Sc in each st around. (18)

Rnd 5: (Sc in next st, sc next 2 sts tog) around, join with sl st in first st. Leave long end for sewing, fasten off. (12)

Head

Rnd 1: With **Cream** (skin color), ch 2, 6 sc in second chain from hook. 6)
Rnd 2: 2 sc in next st around. (12)
Rnd 3: (Sc in next st, 2 sc in next st) around. (18)
Rnd 4: (Sc in next 2 sts, 2 sc in next st) around. (24)
Rnd 5-9: Sc in each st around. (24)
Rnd 10: (Sc in next 2 sts, sc next 2 sts tog) around. (18)
Rnd 11: (Sc in next st, sc next 2 sts tog) around, join with sl st in first st. Fasten off. Stuff. (12)

Arm

Make 2 for each Fairy, do not stuff arms.
Rnd 1: With **Cream** (skin color), ch 2, 6 sc in second chain from hook. (6)
Rnd 2-3: Sc in each st around. (6)
Rnd 4: Sc in each st around, sl st in first st. Fasten off. (6)

Wing

Make two for each Fairy.
With **Green** (wing color), ch 10, sl st in second chain from hook, sc in next ch, hdc in next ch, dc in next 3 chs, hdc in next ch, sc in next ch, sl st in next ch; working in remaining loops on opposite side of chain, sc in next ch, hdc in next ch, dc in next 3 chs, hdc in next ch, sc in next ch, sl st in next ch, leave long end for sewing, fasten off. (18)

Yellow, Orange & Green Fairies

Skirt

Rnd 1: Join **Green** (skirt color) to free loop of rnd 2 of the body, ch 1, sc in same st, sc in each st around. (18)

Rnd 2: (Sc in next st, 3 dc in next st) around, join with sl st in first st, fasten off.

Cap

Rnd 1: With **Green** (cap color), ch 2, 6 sc in second chain from hook. (6)
Rnd 2: 2 sc in next st around. (12)
Rnd 3: (Sc in next st, 2 sc in next st) around. (18)
Rnd 4: (Sc in next 2 sts, 2 sc in next st) around. (24)
Rnd 5: (Sc in next 3 sts, 2 sc in next st) around. (30)
Rnd 6-8: Sc in each st around. (30)
Rnd 9: (Sc in next st, 3 dc in next st, sc in next st) around, join with sl st in first st, leave long end for sewing. Fasten off. (30)

Finishing

Stuff the body and sew head to body. Sew arms to body. Sew eyes 4 - 5 sts apart between rnds 7 - 8. With **Red** embroidery floss, embroider mouth on rnd 9.

Pin cap on head and sew.

Sew wings on middle back of body.

White, Red & Blue Fairies

Skirt

Rnd 1: Join **Blue** (skirt color) to free loop of rnd 2 of the body, ch 1, sc in same st, 2 sc in next st, (sc in next 2 sts, 2 sc in next st) 5 times, sc in next st. (24)

Rnd 2: (Sc in next st, ch 5) around, sl st in first st. Fasten off.

Cap

Working on back loops only.

Rnd 1: With **Blue** (cap color), ch 2, 6 sc in second chain from hook. (6)

Rnd 2: 2 sc in next st around. (12)

Rnd 3: (Sc in next st, 2 sc in next st) around. (18)

Rnd 4: (Sc in next 2 sts, 2 sc in next st) around. (24)

Rnd 5: (Sc in next 3 sts, 2 sc in next st) around. (30)

Rnd 6: Sc in each st around. (30)

Rnd 7: Sc in each st around, join with sl st in first st, leave long end for sewing. Fasten off. (30)

Hair

Working in free loops of the cap.

Join **Blue** (hair color) to free loop of rnd 1 of the cap, ch1, sc in same st, (ch 2, sc in next st) around until cover all the cap. Leave long end for sewing, fasten off.

Finishing

Stuff the body and sew head to body. Sew arms to body. Sew eyes 4 - 5 sts apart between rnds 7 - 8. With **Red** embroider floss, embroider mouth on rnd 9. Pin cap on head and sew. Sew wings on middle back of body.

Pink, Light Purple & Dark Pink Fairies

Skirt

Rnd 1: Join **Dark pink** (skirt color) to free loop of rnd 2 of the body, ch 1, sc in same st, (2 sc in next st, sc in next st) 5 times, 2 sc in next st. (24)

Rnd 2: (Sc in next st, ch 3, dc in next st, ch 3) around, join with sl st in first st, fasten off.

Cap

Rnd 1: With **Dark pink** (cap color), ch 2, 6 sc in second chain from hook. (6)

Rnd 2: 2 sc in next st around. (12)

Rnd 3: (Sc in next st, 2 sc in next st) around. (18)

Rnd 4: (Sc in next 2 sts, 2 sc in next st) around. (24)

Rnd 5: (Sc in next 3 sts, 2 sc in next st) around. (30)

Rnd 6-8: Sc in each st around. (30)

Rnd 9: (Sc in next st, ch 3, dc in next st, ch 3) around, join with sl st in first st, leave long end for sewing. Fasten off. (30)

Finishing

Stuff the body and sew head to body. Sew arms to body. Sew eyes 4 - 5 sts apart between rnds 7-8. With **Red** embroidery floss, embroider mouth on rnd 9. Pin cap on head and sew. Sew wings on middle back of body.

Bride & Groom

Materials

- No 2 yarn (Sport, Baby) 2 fine
  4 ply Acrylic yarn; White = 20 g, Gray = 20 g, Light Pink = 10 g, Cream = 40 g, Black = 10 g, Light Brown = 20 g and a little bit of Light Green, Yellow and Red
- 3.00 mm hook
- Polyester fiberfill = 150 g
- Tapestry needle
- 4 Black 10 mm buttons for eyes or other eyes as desired
- Sewing needle and thread for attaching eyes and hair (thread same color as hair)

Size

Bride: 6 inches (15 cm) tall
Bouquet: 2 inches (5 cm)
Groom: 6.5 inches (16.5 cm) tall

Bride

Foot and Leg

Make 2.

Rnd 1: With **White**, ch 2, 6 sc in second chain from hook. (6 sc made)
Rnd 2: 2 sc in each st around. (12)
Rnd 3: (Sc in next st, 2 sc in next st) around. (18)
Rnd 4: (2 sc in next st, sc in next 2 sts) around. (24)
Rnd 5: Working in back loops only. Sc in each st around.
Rnd 6: Sc in next 10 sts, (sc next 2 sts tog) 4 times, sc in next 6 sts. (20)
Rnd 7: (Sc next 2 sts tog, sc in next 2 sts) 2 times, (sc next 2 sts tog) 5 times, sc in next 2 sts, changing to **Cream** in last 2 loops of last st.Stuff. (13)
Rnd 8-13: Sc in each st around.

For first leg, join with sl st in first st. Fasten off.
For second leg, do not sl st in first st. Do not fasten off.

Body and Head

Rnd 1: Hold legs together with toes pointed forward. Insert hook in the center on innermost thigh of **first leg**, pull out the loop from **second leg**, sc in same st (do not count this st just for connecting legs together), sc in next 12 sts on second leg (mark first st), sc in next 12 sts on first leg. (24)
* See diagram of how to connect legs together on page 44*
Rnd 2: (Sc in next 2 sts, 2 sc in next st) around. Stuff legs. (32)
Rnd 3: Sc in each st around.
Rnd 4: (Sc in next 7 sts, 2sc in next st) around. (36)
Rnd 5-6: Sc in each st around, changing to **White** in last 2 loops of last st.
Rnd 7: Sc in each st around.
Rnd 8: Working in back loops only. Sc in each st around.
Rnd 9: Sc in each st around.
Rnd 10: (Sc next 2 sts tog, sc in next 4 sts) around. (30)
Rnd 11: Sc in next 2 sts, sc next 2 sts tog, (sc in next 3 sts, sc next 2 sts tog) 5 times, sc in next st. (24)
Rnd 12: (Sc next 2 sts tog, sc in next 2 sts) around, changing to **Cream** in last 2 loops of last st. Stuff. (18)
Rnd 13: Working in back loops only. (2 sc in next st, sc in next 2 sts) around. (24)
Rnd 14: Sc in next 5 sts, (2 sc in next st) 3 times, sc in next 9 sts, (2 sc in next st) 3times, sc in next 4 sts. (30)
Rnd 15: Sc in next 5 sts, 2 sc in next st, (sc in next st, 2 sc in next st) 2 times, sc in next 10 sts, 2 sc in next st, (sc in next st, 2 sc in next st) 2 times, sc in next 5 sts. (36)
Rnd 16: Sc in next 6 sts, 2 sc in next st, (sc in next 2 sts, 2sc in next st) 2 times, sc in next 11 sts, 2 sc in next st, (sc in next 2 sts, 2 sc next st) 2 times, sc in next 5 sts. (42)
Rnd 17: Sc in next 6 sts, 2 sc in next st, (sc in next 3 sts, 2 sc in next st) 2 times, sc in next 12 sts, 2 sc in next st, (sc in next 3 sts, 2 sc in next st) 2 times, sc in next 6 sts. (48)
Rnd 18: Sc in each st around.
Rnd 19: (Sc in next 7 sts, 2 sc in next st) around. (54)
Rnd 20: Sc in each st around.
Rnd 21: (Sc in next 8 sts, 2 sc in next st) around. (60)
Rnd 22-26: Sc in each st around.
Rnd 27: Sc in next 4 sts, sc next 2 sts tog, (sc in next 8 sts, sc next 2 sts tog) 5 times, sc in next 4 sts. (54)
Rnd 28: Sc in each st around.
Rnd 29: (Sc in next 7 sts, sc next 2 sts tog) around.(48)

Rnd 30: Sc in each st around.
Rnd 31: Sc in next 3 sts, sc next 2 sts tog, (sc in next 6 sts, sc next 2 sts tog) 5 times, sc in next 3 sts. (42)
Rnd 32: (Sc in next 5 sts, sc next 2 sts tog) around. (36)
Rnd 33: (Sc in next 4 sts, sc next 2 sts tog) around. (30)
Rnd 34: (Sc in next 3 sts, sc next 2 sts tog) around. (24)
Rnd 35: (Sc in next 2 sts, sc next 2 sts tog) around. Stuff. (18)
Rnd 36: (Sc in next st, sc next 2 sts tog) around. (12)
Rnd 37: (Sc next 2 sts tog) around, join with sl st in first st. Fasten off.

Skirt

Rnd 1: Join **White** yarn to free loop of rnd 7 of the body, ch 1, sc in same st, sc in each st around. (36)
Rnd 2-4: Sc in each st around.
Rnd 5: (Sc in next 5 sts, 2 sc in next st) around. (42)
Rnd 6-7: Sc in each st around.
Rnd 8: (Sc in next 6 sts, 2 sc in next st) around. (48)
Rnd 9-11: Sc in each st around.
Rnd 12: (Sc in next 7 sts, 2 sc in next st) around. (54)
Rnd 13-14: Sc in each st around.
Rnd 15: Sc in each st around, changing to **Light pink** in last 2 loops of last st.
Rnd 16: Working in back loops only. Sc in each st around.
Rnd 17: Sc in each st around.
Rnd 18: (2 sc in next st, sc in next 17 sts) around. (57)
Rnd 19-20: Sc in each st around.
Rnd 21: (Sl st in next st, skip next st, 5 dc in next st) around. Fasten off.

Edge of skirt in White color

Rnd 1: Join **White** yarn to free loop of rnd 15, ch 1, sc in same st, sc in each st around. (54)
Rnd 2: Sc in each st around.
Rnd 3: (Sl st in next st, ch 2, 2dc in the same st, skip one st) around. Fasten off.

Bow

Bow piece

Working in rows.

Row 1: With **Light pink**, ch 2, 3 sc in second ch from hook, turn. (3)
Row 2: Ch 1, sc in each st across, turn.
Row 3: Ch 1, 2 sc in first st, sc in next st, 2 sc in next st, turn. (5)
Row 4-8: Ch 1, sc in each st across, turn.
Row 9: Ch 1, sc first 2 sts tog, sc in next st, sc next 2 sts tog, turn. (3)
Row 10-13: Ch 1, sc in each st across, turn.
Row 14: Ch 1, 2 sc in first st, sc in next st, 2 sc in next st, turn. (5)
Row 15-19: Ch 1, sc in each st across, turn.
Row 20: Ch 1, sc first 2 sts tog, sc in next st, sc next 2 sts tog, turn. (3)
Row 21: Ch 1, sc in each st across.
Row 22: Ch 1, sc 3 sts tog, leaving long end for sewing, fasten off. (1)

Middle piece

With **Light pink**, ch 30, sc in second chain from hook, sc in each ch across, fasten off.(29)

Assembly

Sew row 1 and row 22 of bow piece together. Tie a middle piece around middle of bow.

Pink stripe

With **Light pink**, Ch 33, fasten off. Sew over rnd 8 around body.

Sew Bow on stripe on middle back of body.

Arm

Make 2.

Rnd 1: With **White**, ch 2, 6 sc in second chain from hook. (6)

Rnd 2: (2 sc in next st, sc in next st) around. (9)

Rnd 3-9: Sc in each st around.

Rnd 10: (Sc in next 2 sts, 2 sc in next st) around. (12)

Rnd 11: (Sc in next st, ch 3, sc in next st) around. Fasten off.

Hand

Make 2.

Rnd 1: With **Cream**, ch 2, 6 sc in second chain from hook. (6)

Rnd 2: Sc in each st around.

Rnd 3: 2 sc in next st, sc in next 4 sts, 2 sc in next st. (8)

Rnd 4: Sc in each st around.

Rnd 5: Sc in next 3 sts, sc next 2 sts tog, sc in next 3 sts. Fasten off. (7)

Stuff hands and arms. Put rnd 5 of hand inside arm and pin and sew them together.

Sew arms to body.

Bridal Bouquet

Flower

Make 4 pink, 2 light green, 2 yellow.

Ch 4, 4 dc in the first chain, 4 hdc in same ch, leave 1 inch for gathering, fasten off.

Insert hook in the first chain(center), pull out the yarn end tight to gather.

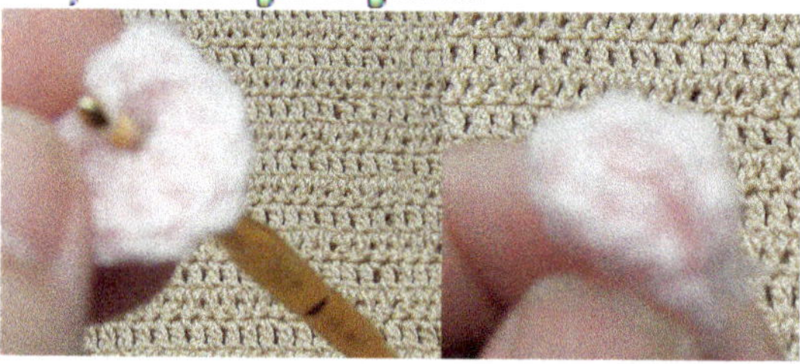

Bouquet

Rnd 1: With **White**, ch 2, 5 sc in second ch from hook. (5)

Rnd 2-7: Sc in each st around.

Rnd 8: 2 sc in each st around. (10)

Rnd 9: 2 sc in each st around. (20)

Rnd 10: (Sl st in next st, skip next st, 5 dc in next st, skip next st) around, fasten off.

Sew flowers together.

Insert hook in the center bottom of bouquet, pull out the yarn end from flowers, pull tight, secure.

Tie a bow on bouquet with colorful yarns (light pink, light green, yellow).

Flowers for hair

Make flowers (same as flowers for bridal bouquet); 2 **Light pink**, one **Yellow** and one **Light green**. Sew them together as in picture, tie with **Light pink** yarn.

Hair

See page 76 if you use DMC Petra or DK yarn.

Draw a line on your doll's head, starting from the left side of forehead to middle top of head and from here to back of head (3-4 rnds from middle top of head).

With **Light brown** and **Brown**, cut them 10 inches (25 cm) long for hair, cut many strands as needed. 4ply yarn means 4 strands of thinner yarn have been twisted together to produce the yarn. Split the yarn to 4 thinner strands to make soft curly thin hair. For **Brown** just use a few strands to highlight the hair.

Hold 6 thin strands of yarn together (five **Light brown** and one **Brown**), fold in half, sew on the line you've drawn earlier on your doll's head, starting from left side of forehead to back of head.

For hair in front; cut 2 strands of **Light brown** and one strand of **Brown** 13 inches (32.5 cm) long, split **Light brown** to 8 thin strands and **Brown** to 4 thin strand. Hold 8 thin strands of **Light brown** and 1 thin strand of **Brown** together, fold in half, sew in the front as picture below and tie together on the back of head, tie flowers on hair and trim.

Finishing

Sew eyes 8 sts apart over rnds 22-23 of head. With **Red**, embroider mouth. Tie flowers on hair.

Groom

Foot and Leg

Make 2.

Rnd 1: With **Black**, ch 2, 6 sc in second chain from hook. (6 sc made)
Rnd 2: 2 sc in each st around. (12)
Rnd 3: (Sc in next st, 2 sc in next st) around. (18)
Rnd 4: (2 sc in next st, sc in next 2 sts) around. (24)
Rnd 5: Working in back loops only. Sc in each st around.
Rnd 6: Sc in next 10 sts, (sc next 2 sts tog) 4 times, sc in next 6 sts.(20)
Rnd 7: (Sc next 2 sts tog, sc in next 2 sts) 2 times, (sc next 2 sts tog) 5 times, sc in next 2 sts, changing to **Cream** in last 2 loops of last st.(13)
Rnd 8: Sc in each st around, changing to **Gray** in last 2 loops of last st.
Rnd 9: Sc in each st around. Stuff.
Rnd 10: Working in back loops only. Sc in each st around.
Rnd 11-13: Sc in each st around.

For first leg, join with sl st in first st. Fasten off.
For second leg, do not sl st in first st. Do not fasten off.

Edge of pants

Rnd 1: Join **Gray** yarn to free loop of rnd 9, ch 1, sc in same st, sc in each st around. (13)
Rnd 2: 2 sc in next st, sc in next 6 sts, 2 sc in next st, sc in next 5 sts, join with sl st in first st. Fasten off.(15)

Body and Head

Rnd 1: Hold legs together with toes pointed forward. Insert hook in the center on innermost thigh of first leg, pull out the loop from second leg, sc in same st (do not count this st just for connecting legs together), sc in next 12 sts on second leg (mark first st), sc in next 12 sts on first leg. (24)
* See diagram of how to connect legs together on page 44*

Rnd 2: (Sc in next 2 sts, 2 sc in next st) around. Stuff legs. (32)
Rnd 3: Sc in each st around.
Rnd 4: (Sc in next 7 sts, 2 sc in next st) around. (36)
Rnd 5: Sc in each st around.
Rnd 6: Working in back loops only. Sc in each st around.
Rnd 7-9: Sc in each st around.
Rnd 10: (Sc next 2 sts tog, sc in next 4 sts) around. (30)
Rnd 11: Sc in next 2 sts, sc next 2 sts tog, (sc in next 3 sts, sc next 2 sts tog) 5 times, sc in next st. (24)
Rnd 12: (Sc next 2 sts tog, sc in next 2 sts) around, changing to **Cream** in last 2 loops of last st. Stuff. (18)
Rnd 13: Working in back loops only. (2 sc in next st, sc in next 2 sts) around. (24)
Rnd 14: Sc in next 5 sts, (2sc in next st) 3 times, sc in next 9 sts, (2 sc in next st) 3 times, sc in next 4 sts. (30)
Rnd 15: Sc in next 5 sts, 2 sc in next st, (sc in next st, 2 sc in next st) 2 times, sc in next 10 sts, 2 sc in next st, (sc in next st, 2 sc in next st) 2 times, sc in next 5 sts. (36)
Rnd 16: Sc in next 6 sts, 2 sc in next st, (sc in next 2 sts, 2sc in next st) 2 times, sc in next 11 sts, 2 sc in next, (sc in next 2 sts, 2 sc next st) 2 times, sc in next 5 sts. (42)

Rnd 17: Sc in next 6 sts, 2 sc in next st, (sc in next 3 sts, 2 sc in next st) 2 times, sc in next 12 sts, 2 sc in next st, (sc in next 3 sts, 2 sc in next st) 2 times, sc in next 6 sts. (48)
Rnd 18: Sc in each st around.
Rnd 19: (Sc in next 7 sts, 2 sc in next st) around. (54)
Rnd 20: Sc in each st around.
Rnd 21: (Sc in next 8 sts, 2 sc in next st) around. (60)
Rnd 22-26: Sc in each st around.
Rnd 27: Sc in next 4 sts, sc next 2 sts tog, (sc in next 8 sts, sc next 2 sts tog) 5 times, sc in next 4 sts. (54)
Rnd 28: Sc in each st around.
Rnd 29: (Sc in next 7 sts, sc next 2 sts tog) around.(48)
Rnd 30: Sc in each st around.
Rnd 31: Sc in next 3 sts, sc next 2 sts tog, (sc in next 6 sts, sc next 2 sts tog) 5 times, sc in next 3 sts. (42)
Rnd 32: (Sc in next 5 sts, sc next 2 sts tog) around. (36)
Rnd 33: (Sc in next 4 sts, sc next 2 sts tog) around. (30)
Rnd 34: (Sc in next 3 sts, sc next 2 sts tog) around. (24)
Rnd 35: (Sc in next 2 sts, sc next 2 sts tog) around. Stuff. (18)
Rnd 36: (Sc in next st, sc next 2 sts tog) around. (12)
Rnd 37: (Sc next 2 sts tog) around, join with sl st in first st. Fasten off.

Edge of shirt

Rnd 1: Join **Gray** yarn to free loop of rnd 5 of the body, ch 1, sc in same st, sc in each st around. (36)
Rnd 2: Sc in each st around.
Rnd 3: Sc in each st around, join with sl st in first st. Fasten off.

Bow tie

Bow

Working in rows.
Row 1: With **Light pink**, ch 2, 2 sc in second chain from hook, turn. (2)
Row 2-7: Ch 1, sc in first 2 sts, turn. (2)
Row 8: Ch 1, sc first 2 sts tog, turn. (1)
Row 9: Ch 1, 2 sc in first st, turn. (2)
Row 10-15: Ch 1, sc in first 2 sts, turn. (2)
Row 16: Ch 1, sc first 2 sts tog, fasten off. (1)
Sew row 1 and row 16 together.

Middle piece

Ch 4, leave long end for sewing, fasten off.
Sew the middle piece around middle of bow.

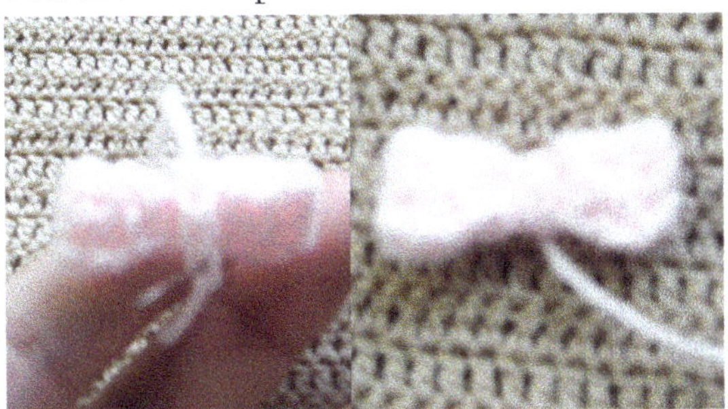

Sew bow on middle front of the body (rnd 12 of body).

Arm

Make 2.
Rnd 1: With **Gray**, ch 2, 6 sc in second chain from hook. (6)
Rnd 2: (2 sc in next st, sc in next st) around. (9)
Rnd 3-8: Sc in each st around.
Rnd 9: Sc in each st around, changing to **Cream** in last 2 loops of last st.
Rnd 10: Working in back loops only.
Sc in next 3 sts, sc next 2 sts tog, sc in next 4 sts. (8)
Rnd 11: Sc in each st around. Stuff.
Rnd 12: (Sc next 2 sts tog, sc in next 2 sts) 2 times, join with sl st in first st. Fasten off. (6)
Sew arms to body.

Hair

See page 76 if you use DMC Petra or DK yarn.
With **Light brown**, cut yarn 10 inches (25 cm) long for hair, cut many strands as needed. Split the yarn to 4 thinner strands to make soft curly thin hair.

For hair, hold 2 strands of yarn, fold in half, with top of the head facing, insert hook toward middle top of head in rnd 9 from middle top of head, draw the folded end through the stitch and pull the loose ends through the folded end, draw the knot up tightly.

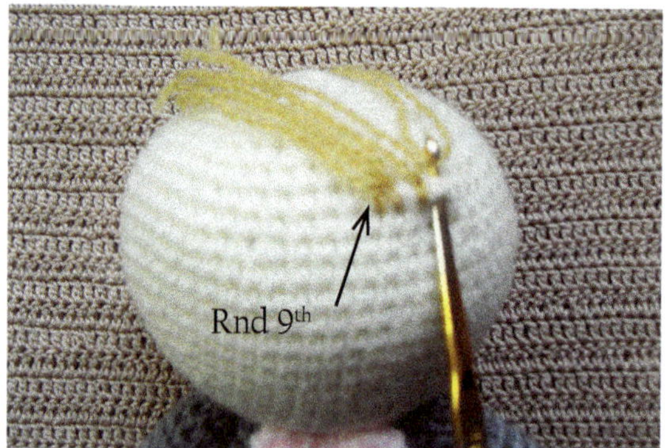

Add hair around up to middle of the head on rnd 7, 5, 3, 2, 1 from middle top of head. Trim hair.

Finishing

Sew eyes 8 sts apart over rnds 22-23 of head. With **Red**, embroider mouth.

Cute Couple

Materials

2 fine

- No 2 yarn (Sport, Baby)
  4 ply Acrylic yarn; Cream = 10 g, Green = 30 g, Light blue = 10 g, Blue =5 g, Red = 5 g, Yellow = 5 g, Pink = 10 g, Light pink = 5 g and Light brown = 20 g
- 3.00 mm hook
- Black embroidery floss
- Polyester fiberfill = 100 g
- Four 4 mm black beads for eyes
- Thirteen 4 mm white beads (for decorating flowers)
- Tapestry needle
- Sewing needle and thread for attaching eyes and flowers

Size

Boy and Girl are 3 inches/ 7.5 cm high in sitting position
Grass base diameter: 4.5 inches/ 11 cm, high: 2 inches/ 5 cm
Small Heart wide: 1.8 inches/ 4.5 cm, high: 1.5 inches/ 4 cm

Small Heart

Hump

Make 2.

Rnd 1: With **Red**, ch 2, 6 sc in second chain from hook. (6)

Rnd 2: 2 sc in each st around. (12)
Rnd 3: Sc in each st around.

For first hump, join with sl st in first st. Fasten off.
For second hump, do not sl st in first st. Do not fasten off.

Rnd 4: With the right side facing you, sc in st on first hump (mark first st), sc in next 11 sts on first hump, sc in next 12 sts on second hump. (24)

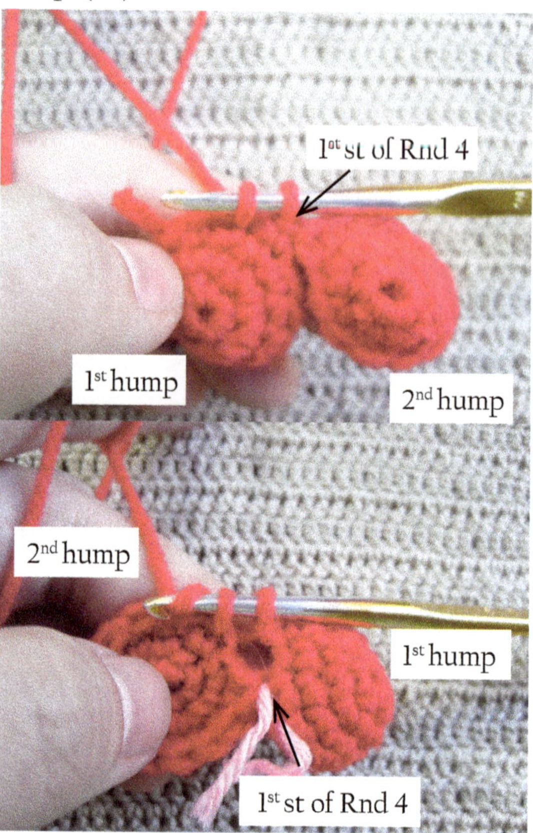

Rnd 5: Sc in each st around. (24)
Rnd 6: (Sc in next 4 sts, sc next 2 sts tog) around. (20)
Rnd 7: (Sc in next 3 sts, sc next 2 sts tog) around. (16)
Rnd 8: (Sc in next 2 sts, sc next 2 sts tog) around. Stuff. (12)
Rnd 9: (Sc in next st, sc next 2 sts tog) around. (8)
Rnd 10: (Sc next 2 sts tog) around, join with sl st in first st. Fasten off. (4)
Sew all openings close.

Girl

Head & Body

Work from bottom of body to top of head.

Rnd 1: With **Light pink**, ch 2, 6 sc in second chain from hook. (6)
Rnd 2: 2 sc in each st around. (12)
Rnd 3: (Sc in next st, 2 sc in next st) around. (18)
Rnd 4: (Sc in next 2 sts, 2 sc in next st) around. (24)
Rnd 5: Sc in next 2 sts, (sc next 2 sts tog, sc in next 5 sts) 3 times, sc in next st. (21)
Rnd 6: Sc in each st around.
Rnd 7: Working in back loops only. Sc in each st around.
Rnd 8: (Sc in next 5 sts, sc next 2 sts tog) around. (18)
Rnd 9: Sc in each st around.
Rnd 10: (Sc next 2 sts tog, sc in next st) around, changing to **Cream** in last 2 loops of last st. (12)
Rnd 11: (2 sc in next st, sc in next st) around. (18)
Rnd 12: (Sc in next 2 sts, 2 sc in next st) around. (24)
Rnd 13: Sc in next st, 2 sc in next st, (sc in next 3 sts, 2 sc in next st) 5 times, sc in next 2 sts. (30)
Rnd 14: (Sc in next 4 sts, 2 sc in next st) around. (36)
Rnd 15-18: Sc in each st around.
Rnd 19: (Sc next 2 sts tog, sc in next 4 sts) around, changing to **Light brown** (hair color) in last 2 loops of last st. (30)
Rnd 20: Sc in next 2 sts, sc next 2 sts tog, (sc in next 3 sts, sc next 2 sts tog) 5 times, sc in next st. (24)

Rnd 21-23: Working in back loops only.

Rnd 21: (Sc next 2 sts tog, sc in next 2 sts) around. Stuff. (18)
Rnd 22: (Sc in next st, sc next 2 sts tog) around. (12)
Rnd 23: Sc next 2 sts tog around, sl st in first st. Fasten off. Sew opening close. (6)

Skirt

Rnd 1: Join **Light pink** to free loop of rnd 6, ch 1, sc in same st, sc in each st around. (21)

Rnd 2: 2 sc in each st around. (42)
Rnd 3: Sc in each st around, join with sl st in first st. Fasten off.

Arm

Make 2, do not stuff arms.

Rnd 1: With **Cream**, ch 2, 6 sc in second chain from hook. (6)

Rnd 2-6: Sc in each st around.

Rnd 7: Sc in each st around, sl st in first st. Fasten off. Sew arms to body.

Leg

Make 2, do not stuff legs

Rnd 1: With **Cream**, ch 2, 6 sc in second chain from hook. (6)

Rnd 2-5: Sc in each st around, join with sl st in first st. Fasten off.

Sew legs to body on rnd 3.

Small flower

Make 1.

With **Pink,** ch 6, sl st in first chain*, (ch 5, sl st in first ch*) 4 times, fasten off.

*same chain, the first starting chain.

Hair

See page 76 if you use DMC Petra or DK yarn.

With **Light brown,** cut yarn 7 inches (17.5 cm) long for hair, cut as many strands as needed. To make thin hair: 4ply yarn means 4 strands of thinner yarn have been twisted together to produce the yarn.

Split the yarn to 2 thinner strands (one thinner strand has 2 single strands twisted together).

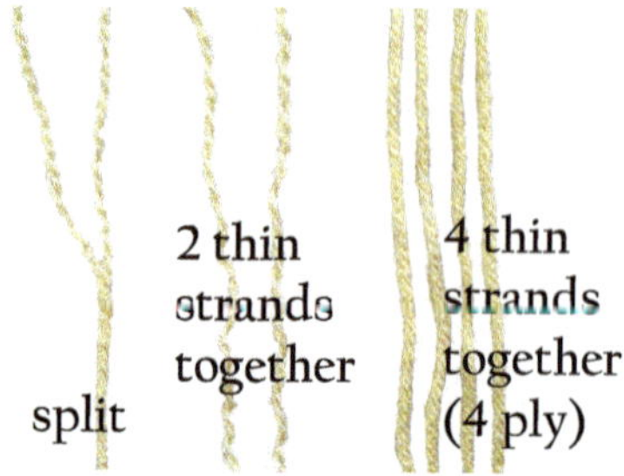

For hair, hold one strand of yarn, fold in half, with top of the head facing, insert hook towards outer of head in free loops on rnds 20-22 and in middle top of head, draw the folded end through the stitch and pull the loose ends through the folded end, draw the knot up tightly.

Finishing

Sew eyes 8 sts apart between rnds 16-17 of head. With **Black** embroidery floss, embroider eyelashes. With **Red**, embroider mouth on rnd 15.

Sew flower on right side of head with white bead in the middle as shown in picture.

Boy

Head & Body

Rnd 1: With **Blue**, ch 2, 6 sc in second chain from hook. (6)
Rnd 2: 2 sc in each st around. (12)
Rnd 3: (Sc in next st, 2 sc in next st) around. (18)
Rnd 4: (Sc in next 2 sts, 2 sc in next st) around. (24)
Rnd 5: Sc in next 2 sts, (sc next 2 sts tog, sc in next 5 sts) 3 times, sc in next st. (21)
Rnd 6: Sc in each st around, changing to **Light blue** in last 2 loops of last st.
Rnd 7: Sc in each st around.
Rnd 8: (Sc in next 5 sts, sc next 2 sts tog) around. (18)
Rnd 9: Sc in each st around.
Rnd 10: (Sc next 2 sts tog, sc in next st) around, changing to **Cream** in last 2 loops of last st. (12)
Rnd 11: (2 sc in next st, sc in next st) around. (18)
Rnd 12: (Sc in next 2 sts, 2 sc in next st) around. (24)
Rnd 13: Sc in next st, (2 sc in next st, sc in next 3 sts) 5 times, 2 sc in next st, sc in next 2 sts. (30)
Rnd 14: (Sc in next 4 sts, 2 sc in next st) around. (36)
Rnd 15-18: Sc in each st around.
Rnd 19: (Sc next 2 sts tog, sc in next 4 sts) around, changing to **Light brown** (hair color) in last 2 loops of last st. (30)
Rnd 20: Sc in next 2 sts, sc next 2 sts tog, (sc in next 3 sts, sc next 2 sts tog) 5 times, sc in next st. (24)

Rnd 21-23: Working in back loops only.
Rnd 21: (Sc next 2 sts tog, sc in next 2 sts) around. Stuff. (18)
Rnd 22: (Sc in next st, sc next 2 sts tog) around. (12)
Rnd 23: Sc next 2 sts tog around, sl st in first st. Fasten off. Sew opening close. (6)

Arm

Make 2, do not stuff arms
Rnd 1: With **Cream**, ch 2, 6 sc in second chain from hook. (6)
Rnd 2: Sc in each st around, changing to **Light blue** in last 2 loops of last st.
Rnd 3-6: Sc in each st around.
Rnd 7: Sc in each st around, sl st in first st. Fasten off. Sew arms to body.

Leg

Make 2, do not stuff legs.
Rnd 1: With **Cream**, ch 2, 6 sc in second chain from hook. (6)
Rnd 2: Sc in each st around, changing to **Blue** in last 2 loops of last st.
Rnd 3-4: Sc in each st around.
Rnd 5: Sc in each st around, join with sl st in first st, fasten off. Sew legs to body on rnd 3 same as the Girl.

Hair

Do the same as the Girl's hair and then cut the hair short.

Finishing

Sew eyes 8 sts apart between rnds 16-17 of head. With **Red**, embroider mouth on rnd 15.

Grass Base

Grass Base

Rnd 1: With **Green**, ch 2, 6 sc in second chain from hook. (6)
Rnd 2: 2 sc in each st around. (12)
Rnd 3: (Sc in next st, 2 sc in next st) around. (18)
Rnd 4: (Sc in next 2 sts, 2 sc in next st) around. (24)
Rnd 5: (Sc in next 3 sts, 2 sc in next st) around. (30)
Rnd 6: (Sc in next 4 sts, 2 sc in next st) around. (36)
Rnd 7: (Sc in next 5 sts, 2 sc in next st) around. (42)
Rnd 8: (Sc in next 6 sts, 2 sc in next st) around. (48)
Rnd 9: (Sc in next 7 sts, 2 sc in next st) around. (54)
Rnd 10: (Sc in next 8 sts, 2 sc in next st) around. (60)
Rnd 11: (Sc in next 9 sts, 2 sc in next st) around. (66)
Rnd 12: (Sc in next 10 sts, 2 sc in next st) around. (72)
Rnd 13: (Sc in next 11 sts, 2 sc in next st) around. (78)
Rnd 14: (Sc in next 12 sts, 2 sc in next st) around. (84)
Rnd 15: Sc in each st around.
Rnd 16: (Sc in next 13 sts, 2 sc in next st) around. (90)
Rnd 17: Sc in each st around.
Rnd 18: (Sc in next 14 sts, 2 sc in next st) around. (96)
Rnd 19: Sc in each st around.
Rnd 20: (Sc next 15 sts, 2 sc in next st) around. (102)
Rnd 21: Sc in each st around.
Rnd 22: Working in back loops only. (Sc in next 15 sts, sc next 2 sts tog) around. (96)
Rnd 23: (Sc in next 6 sts, sc next 2 sts tog) around. (84)
Rnd 24: (Sc in next 5 sts, sc next 2 sts tog) around. (72)
Rnd 25: (Sc in next 10 sts, sc next 2 sts tog) around. (66)
Rnd 26: (Sc in next 9 sts, sc next 2 sts tog) around. (60)
Rnd 27: (Sc in next 8 sts, sc next 2 sts tog) around. (54)
Rnd 28: (Sc in next 7 sts, sc next 2 sts tog) around. (48)
Rnd 29: (Sc in next 6 sts, sc next 2 sts tog) around. (42)
Rnd 30: (Sc in next 5 sts, sc next 2 sts tog) around. (36)
Rnd 31: (Sc in next 4 sts, sc next 2 sts tog) around. (30)
Rnd 32: (Sc in next 3 sts, sc next 2 sts tog) around. Stuff not to tight. (24)
Rnd 33: (Sc in next 2 sts, sc next 2 sts tog) around. (18)
Rnd 34: (Sc in next st, sc next 2 sts tog) around. (12)
Rnd 35: (Sc next 2 sts tog) around, join with sl st in first st, fasten off. Sew opening close. (6)

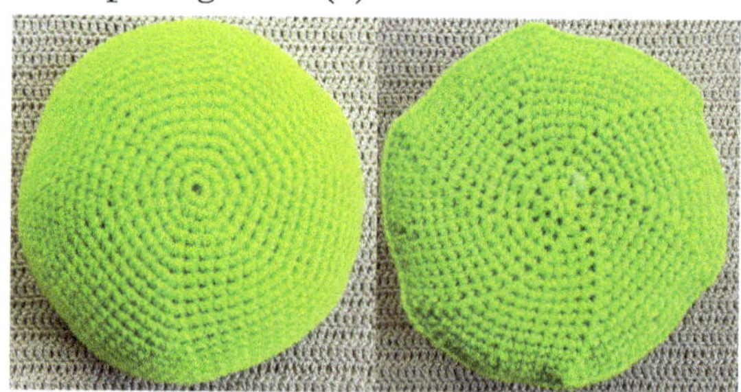

Flower

Make 4 each in yellow, pink and light blue.

Rnd 1: With **Green**. Ch 4, join to form a ring, ch 1, 12 sc in a ring, changing to **Pink** in last 2 loops of last st. (12)

Rnd 2: (Sc in next st, ch 2, 4 dc in next st, ch 2) 6 times, join with sl st to first st, fasten off.

Sew flowers on rnd 20 of Grass Base with white bead in the middle, as shown in picture.

Finishing

Sew Boy and Girl on middle top of Grass Base and sew a heart to one of their hands. You can put only one doll on top of the Grass Base too.

Heart Cushion

Materials

- No 5 yarn (Bulky, Chunky) Robin Chunky yarn; Red = 200 g
- 5.5 mm hook (US = I, UK = 5)
- Tapestry needle
- Polyester fiberfill = 500 gm

5 Bulky

Sizes

Heart cushion: Wide: 16 inches/ 40 cm
High: 11 inches/ 27.5 cm tall

Gauge

5.5 mm hook: 4 sc = 1 inch, 4 rows = 1 inch
(1 inch is 2.5 cm)

This pattern can be made using any yarn you wish. Choose a hook size that matches the yarn. If you use thinner yarn and smaller hook, the heart will be smaller. If you use thicker yarn and bigger hook, it will be bigger.

Heart

Hump (make 2).

Rnd 1: With **Red**, ch 2, 6 sc in second chain from hook. (6)
Rnd 2: 2 sc in each st around. (12)
Rnd 3: (Sc in next st, 2 sc in next st) around. (18)
Rnd 4: Sc in next st, 2 sc in next st, (sc in next 2 sts, 2 sc in next st) 5 times, sc in next st. (24)
Rnd 5: (Sc in next 3 sts, 2 sc in next st) around. (30)
Rnd 6: Sc in next 2 sts, 2 sc in next st, (sc in next 4 sts,2 sc in next st) 5 times, sc in next 2 sts.(36)
Rnd 7: (Sc in next 5 sts, 2 sc in next st) around. (42)
Rnd 8: Sc in next 3 sts, 2 sc in next st, (sc in next 6 sts, 2 sc in next st) 5 times, sc in next 3 sts. (48)
Rnd 9: (Sc in next 7 sts, 2 sc in next st) around. (54)
Rnd 10: Sc in next 4 sts, 2 sc in next st, (sc in next 8 sts, 2 sc in next st) 5 times, sc in next 4 sts. (60)
Rnd 11: (Sc in next 9 sts, 2 sc in next st) around. (66)
Rnd 12: Sc in next 5 sts, 2 sc in next st, (sc in next 10 sts, 2 sc in next st) 5 times, sc in next 5 sts. (72)
Rnd 13: (Sc in next 11 sts, 2 sc in next st) around. (78)
Rnd 14: Sc in each st around.
Rnd 15: Sc in next 6 sts, 2 sc in next st, (sc in next 12 sts, 2 sc in next st) 5 times, sc in next 6 sts. (84)
Rnd 16: Sc in each st around.

For first hump, join with sl st in first st. Fasten off.
For second hump, do not sl st in first st. Do not fasten off.

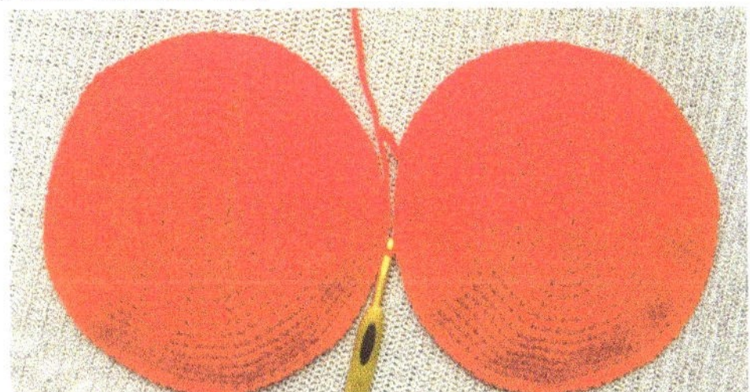

Join the Humps together:

Rnd 17: With the right side facing you, sc in st on first hump (mark first st), sc in next 83 sts on first hump, sc in next 84 sts on second hump. (168)

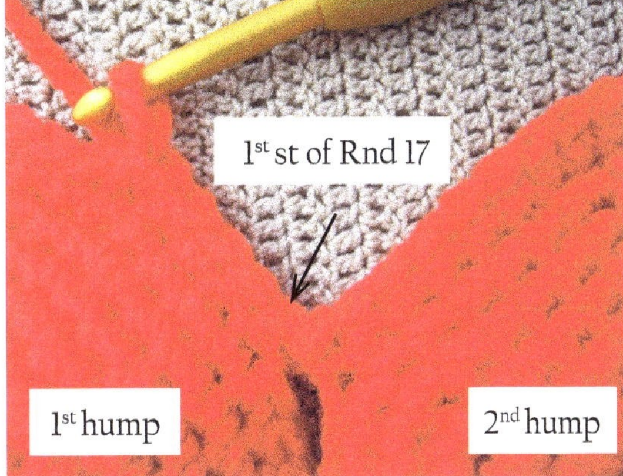

Rnd 18-19: Sc in each st around. (168)
Rnd 20: Sc in next 20 sts, sc next 2 sts tog, (sc in next 40 sts, sc next 2 sts tog) 3 times, sc in next 20 sts. (164)
Rnd 21: (Sc in next 39 sts, sc next 2 sts tog) around. (160)
Rnd 22: Sc in next 19 sts, sc next 2 sts tog, (sc in next 38 sts, sc next 2 sts tog) 3 times, sc in next 19 sts. (156)
Rnd 23: (Sc in next 37 sts, sc next 2 sts tog) around. (152)
Rnd 24: Sc in next 18 sts, sc next 2 sts tog, (sc in next 36 sts, sc next 2 sts tog) 3 times, sc in next 18 sts. (148)
Rnd 25: (Sc in next 35 sts, sc next 2 sts tog) around. (144)
Rnd 26: Sc in next 17 sts, sc next 2 sts tog, (sc in next 34 sts, sc next 2 sts tog) 3 times, sc in next 17 sts. (140)
Rnd 27: (Sc in next 33 sts, sc next 2 sts tog) around. (136)
Rnd 28: Sc in next 16 sts, sc next 2 sts tog, (sc in next 32 sts, sc next 2 sts tog) 3 times, sc in next 16 sts. (132)
Rnd 29: (Sc in next 31 sts, sc next 2 sts tog) around. (128)
Rnd 30: Sc in next 15 sts, sc next 2 sts tog, (sc in next 30 sts, sc next 2 sts tog) 3 times, sc in next 15 sts. (124)
Rnd 31: (Sc in next 29 sts, sc next 2 sts tog) around. (120)

Rnd 32: Sc in next 14 sts, sc next 2 sts tog, (sc in next 28 sts, sc next 2 sts tog) 3 times, sc in next 14 sts. (116)
Rnd 33: (Sc in next 27 sts, sc next 2 sts tog) around. (112)
Rnd 34: Sc in next 13 sts, sc next 2 sts tog, (sc in next 26 sts, sc next 2 sts tog) 3 times, sc in next 13 sts. (108)
Rnd 35: (Sc in next 25 sts, sc next 2 sts tog) around. (104)
Rnd 36: Sc in next 12 sts, sc next 2 sts tog, (sc in next 24 sts, sc next 2 sts tog) 3 times, sc in next 12 sts. (100)
Rnd 37: (Sc in next 23 sts, sc next 2 sts tog) around. (96)
Rnd 38: Sc in next 11 sts, sc next 2 sts tog, (sc in next 22 sts, sc next 2 sts tog) 3 times, sc in next 11 sts. (92)
Rnd 39: (Sc in next 21 sts, sc next 2 sts tog) around. (88)
Rnd 40: Sc in next 10 sts, sc next 2 sts tog, (sc in next 20 sts, sc next 2 sts tog) 3 times, sc in next 10 sts. (84)
Rnd 41: (Sc in next 19 sts, sc next 2 sts tog) around. (80)
Rnd 42: Sc in next 9 sts, sc next 2 sts tog, (sc in next 18 sts, sc next 2 sts tog) 3 times, sc in next 9 sts. (76)
Rnd 43: (Sc in next 17 sts, sc next 2 sts tog) around. (72)
Rnd 44: Sc in next 8 sts, sc next 2 sts tog, (sc in next 16 sts, sc next 2 sts tog) 3 times, sc in next 8 sts. (68)
Rnd 45: (Sc in next 15 sts, sc next 2 sts tog) around. (64)
Rnd 46: Sc in next 7 sts, sc next 2 sts tog, (sc in next 14 sts, sc next 2 sts tog) 3 times, sc in next 7 sts. (60)
Rnd 47: (Sc in next 13 sts, sc next 2 sts tog) around. (56)
Rnd 48: Sc in next 6 sts, sc next 2 sts tog, (sc in next 12 sts, sc next 2 sts tog) 3 times, sc in next 6 sts. (52)
Rnd 49: (Sc in next 11 sts, sc next 2 sts tog) around. (48)
Rnd 50: Sc in next 5 sts, sc next 2 sts tog, (sc in next 10 sts, sc next 2 sts tog) 3 times, sc in next 5 sts. (44)
Rnd 51: (Sc in next 9 sts, sc next 2 sts tog) around. (40)
Rnd 52: Sc in next 4 sts, sc next 2 sts tog, (sc in next 8 sts, sc next 2 sts tog) 3 times, sc in next 4 sts. (36)
Rnd 53: (Sc in next 7 sts, sc next 2 sts tog) around. Stuff; put heart flat on table and stuff not to tight otherwise the heart will be too hard and heavy. (32)
Rnd 54: Sc in next 3 sts, sc next 2 sts tog, (sc in next 6 sts, sc next 2 sts tog) 3 times, sc in next 3 sts. (28)
Rnd 55: (Sc in next 5 sts, sc next 2 sts tog) around. (24)
Rnd 56: Sc in next 2 sts, sc next 2 sts tog, (sc in next 4 sts, sc next 2 sts tog) 3 times, sc in next 2 sts. Stuff. (20)
Rnd 57: (Sc in next 3 sts, sc next 2 sts tog) around. (16)
Rnd 58: Sc in next st, sc next 2 sts tog, (sc in next 2 sts, sc next 2 sts tog) 3 times, sc in next st. (12)
Rnd 59: Sc next 2 sts tog around, join with sl st in first st. Fasten off. (6)

Finishing

Sew the opening between humps close.

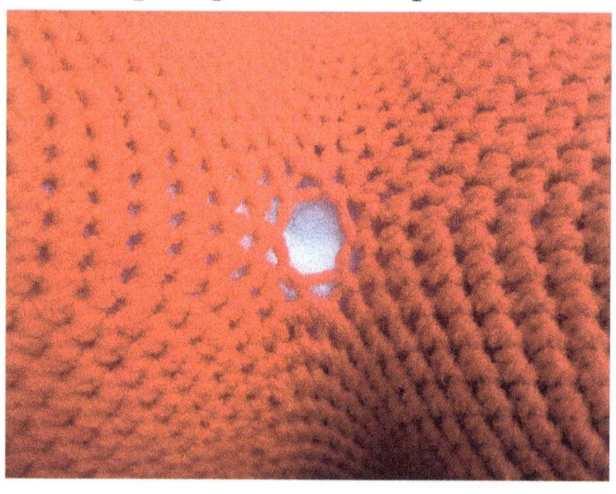

Flower Princess

Materials

2 Fine

- No 2 yarn (Sport, Baby)
  Catania yarn from Schachenmayr SMC;
  Dark blue = 20 g, Blue = 20 g, Jade = 20 g,
  Apple green = 30 g, Yellow = 40 g,
  Orange = 30 g, Red = 30 g and Cream = 10 g
- 3.00 mm hook
- Polyester fiberfill = 20 g
- One pair of 6 mm black safety eyes
- Tapestry needle
- 30 of 4mm white beads for decorate hair
- Pins

Size

The Flower Princess is 10 inches / 25 cm tall.

Foot & Leg

Make 2, only stuff feet, do not stuff legs.

Rnd 1: With **Red**, ch 5, sc in second chain from hook, sc in next 2 chs, 3 sc in last ch; working in remaining loops on opposite side of chain, sc in next 2 chs, 2 sc in next ch. (10)

	x	x	x	x	o
x	o	o	o	o	x
	x	x	x	x	

o = chain x = sc

Rnd 2: 2 sc in next st, sc in next 2 sts, 2 sc in next 3 sts, sc in next 2 sts, 2 sc in next 2 sts. (16)
Rnd 3: 2 sc in next st, sc in next 3 sts, (2 sc in next st, sc in next st) 3 times, sc in next 2 sts, (2 sc in next st, sc in next st) 2 times. (22)
Rnd 4: Working in back loops only. Sc in each st around. (22)
Rnd 5: Sc in each st around. (22)
Rnd 6: Sc in next 4 sts, (sc next 2 sts tog) 5 times, sc in next 8 sts. (17)
Rnd 7: Sc in next 3 sts, sc next 2 sts tog, sc next 3 sts tog, sc next 2 sts tog, sc in next 7 sts. (13)
Rnd 8: Sc next 2 sts tog, sc in next 5 sts, (sc next 2 sts tog) 3 times. (9)
Rnd 9: Working in front loops only. (Ch 2, sc in next st) 9 times, fasten off.

Rnd 10: Join **Apple green** yarn to free loop of rnd 8, ch 1, sc in same st, sc in each st around. Stuff foot. (9)

Rnd 11-40: Sc in each st around. (9)
Rnd 41: Sc in each st around, join with sl st in first st. Fasten off. (9)

This doll has wobbly legs. You can insert iron wire inside legs to make it more sturdy.

Body & Head

Rnd 1: With **Red**, ch 2, 6 sc in second chain from hook. (6)
Rnd 2: 2 sc in each st around. (12)
Rnd 3: (Sc in next st, 2 sc in next st) around. (18)
Rnd 4: (2 sc in next st, sc in next 2 sts) around. (24)
Rnd 5: (Sc in next 3 sts, 2 sc in next sts) around. (30)
Rnd 6-10: Sc in each st around. (30)
Rnd 11: Sc in next 4 sts, (sc next 2 sts tog, sc in next 8 sts) 2 times, sc next 2 sts tog, sc in next 4 sts. (27)
Rnd 12: Sc in each st around, changing to **Orange** in last 2 loops of last st. (27)
Rnd 13: Working in back loops only. Sc in each st around. (27)
Rnd 14: (Sc next 2 sts tog, sc in next 7 sts) around. (24)
Rnd 15: Sc in each st around. (24)
Rnd 16: Sc in each st around, changing to **Yellow** in last 2 loops of last st. (24)
Rnd 17: Sc in next 3 sts, (sc next 2 sts tog, sc in next 6 sts) 2 times, sc next 2 sts tog, sc in next 3 sts. (21)
Rnd 18-19: Sc in each st around. (21)
Rnd 20: (Sc next 2 sts tog, sc in next 5 sts) around, changing to **Apple green** in last 2 loops of last st. (18)
Rnd 21-22: Sc in each st around. (18)

Rnd 23: Sc in next 2 sts, (sc next 2 sts tog, sc in next 4 sts) 2 times, sc next 2 sts tog, sc in next 2 sts. (15)
Rnd 24: Sc in each st around. (15)
Rnd 25: (Sc next 2 sts tog, sc in next 3 sts) around, changing to **Cream** in last 2 loops of last st. (12)
Rnd 26: 2 sc in each st around. (24)
Rnd 27: (Sc in next st, 2 sc in next st) around. Stuff. (36)
Rnd 28-36: Sc in each st around. (36)
Rnd 37: (Sc next 2 sts tog, sc in next 4 sts) around. (30)
Rnd 38: (Sc next 2 sts tog, sc in next 3 sts) around. (24)
Rnd 39: (Sc next 2 sts tog, sc in next 2 sts) around. (18)

Put eyes 5-6 sts apart over rnds 31-32. Stuff. With **Red** embroider mouth on rnd 29.

Rnd 40: (Sc next 2 sts tog, sc in next st) around. (12)
Rnd 41: (Sc next 2 sts tog) around, join with sl st in first st. Fasten off. (6)
Sew legs to the body on rnd 7 of body.

Petal Skirt

Petals

Make 6.

Rnd 1: With **Red**, ch 5, sc in second chain from hook, sc in next 2 chs, 3 sc in last ch; working in remaining loops on opposite side of chain, sc in next 2 chs, 2 sc in next ch. (10)

	x	x	x	x	o
x	o	o	o	o	x
	x	x	x	x	

o = chain x = sc

Rnd 2: 2 sc in next st, sc in next 2 sts, 2 sc in next 3 sts, sc in next 2 sts, 2 sc in next 2 sts. (16)
Rnd 3: 2 sc in next st, sc in next 3 sts, (2 sc in next st, sc in next st) 3 times, sc in next 2 sts, (2 sc in next st, sc in next st) 2 times. (22)
Rnd 4: Sc in next 2 sts, 2 sc in next st, sc in next 4 sts, (2 sc in next st, sc in next 2 sts) 2 times, 2 sc in next st, sc in next 4 sts, 2 sc in next st, sc in next 2 sts, 2 sc in next st, changing to **Orange** in last two loops of last st. (28)
Rnd 5-6: Sc in each st around. (28)
Rnd 7: Sc in each st around, changing to **Yellow** in last two loops of last st. (28)
Rnd 8-9: Sc in each st around. (28)
Rnd 10: (Sc next 2 sts tog, sc in next 12 sts) 2 times, changing to **Apple green** in last two loops of last st. (26)
Rnd 11: Sc in each st around. (26)
Rnd 12: (Sc next 2 sts tog, sc in next 11 sts) 2 times. (24)
Rnd 13: Sc in each st around, changing to **Jade** in last two loops of last st. (24)
Rnd 14: (Sc next 2 sts tog, sc in next 10 sts) 2 times. (22)
Rnd 15: Sc in each st around. (22)
Rnd 16: (Sc next 2 sts tog, sc in next 9 sts) 2 times, changing to **Blue** in last two loops of last st. (20)
Rnd 17: Sc in each st around. (20)
Rnd 18: (Sc next 2 sts tog, sc in next 8 sts) 2 times. (18)
Rnd 19: Sc in each st around, changing to **Dark blue** in last two loops of last st. (18)

Rnd 20: (Sc next 2 sts tog, sc in next 7 sts) 2 times. (16)
Rnd 21: Sc in each st around. (16)
Rnd 22: (Sc next 2 sts tog, sc in next 6 sts) 2 times, changing to **Red** in last two loops of last st. (14)
Rnd 23: Sc in each st around. (14)
Rnd 24: (Sc next 2 sts tog, sc in next 5 sts) 2 times. (12)
Rnd 25: Sc in each st around, join with sl st in first st, fasten off. (12)

Sew Petal Skirt on rnd 12 of body.

Arm

Make 2, do not stuff arms.

Rnd 1: With **Cream**, ch 2, 6 sc in second chain from hook. (6)
Rnd 2-14: Sc in each st around. (6)

See diagram for hand and thumb below.

Rnd 15: For thumb, 2 sc in first st, skip next 4 sts, 2 sc in next st, join with sl st in first st. Fasten off.

Rnd 15: For hand, join **Cream** to the next free st on rnd 14, ch 1, 2 sc in same st, 2 sc in next 3 sts. (8)
Rnd 16: Sc in each st around. (8)
Row 17: Working in rows, flatten last rnd, matching sts and working through both thicknesses, sc in next 2 sts, sl st in next st. Fasten off.

Row 17				cxx		
Rnd 16		xx	xx	xx	xx	
Rnd 15	v	v	v	v	v	v
Rnd 14	x	x	x	x	x	x

Pink = hand
Black = thumb

x = sc
v = 2 sc in same st
c = slip stitch

Sew arms to body on rnds 22-23 with thumbs towards front.

Hair

Hair Cap

Rnd 1: With **Yellow**. Ch 2, 6 sc in second ch from hook. (6)
Rnd 2: 2 sc in each st around. (12)
Rnd 3: (Sc in next st, 2 sc in next st) around. (18)
Rnd 4: (Sc in next 2 sts, 2 sc in next st) around. (24)
Rnd 5: (2 sc in next st, sc in next 3 sts) around. (30)
Rnd 6: (Sc in next 4 sts, 2 sc in next st) around. (36)
Rnd 7: (2 sc in next st, sc in next 5 sts) around.(42)
Rnd 8-12: Sc in each st around.
Row 13: **Hair**; working in row. (Ch 20, sc in second ch from hook, sc in next 18 chs, sc in next st on rnd 12) 31 times, fasten off.

Hair Bun

Rnd 1: With **Yellow**. Ch 2, 6 sc in second ch from hook. (6)
Rnd 2: 2 sc in each st around. (12)
Rnd 3: (Sc in next st, 2 sc in next st) around. (18)
Rnd 4: (Sc in next 2 sts, 2 sc in next st) around. (24)
Rnd 5-7: Sc in each st around.
Rnd 8: Sc in each st around, join with sl st in first st. Fasten off.

Finishing

Sew hair cap on head. Sew hair bun on middle top of head and stuff before sewing the opening close. Sew white beads around hair bun.

Rainbow Girl

Materials

- No 2 yarn (Sport, Baby) 2 Fine
  4 ply Acrylic yarn; Light brown = 10 g, Purple = 15 g, Dark blue = 15 g, Blue = 15 g, Green = 15 g, Yellow = 20 g, Orange = 15 g, Red = 15 g and Dark brown = 15 g
- 3.00 mm hook
- Black embroidery floss
- Polyester fiberfill = 20 g
- Ten 4 mm white beads (for decorating flower)
- Two 4 mm back beads (for eyes)
- Tapestry needle
- Sewing needle and thread for attaching eyes and beads on flowers
- Pins

Size

The Rainbow Girl is 7.5 inches / 19.5 cm tall.

Foot & Leg

Make 2.

Rnd 1: With **Red**, ch 2, 6 sc in second ch from hook. (6)
Rnd 2: 2 sc in each st around. (12)
Rnd 3: (Sc in next st, 2 sc in next st) around. (18)
Rnd 4: Working in back loops only. Sc in each st around.
Rnd 5: Sc in next 6 sts, (sc next 2 sts tog) 3 times, sc in next 6 sts, changing to **Light brown** in last 2 loops of last st. (15)
Rnd 6: Sc in next 3 sts, (sc next 2 sts tog) 2 times, sc in next st, (sc next 2 sts tog) 2 times, sc in next 3 sts. (11)
Rnd 7-12: Sc in each st around. Stuff.
Rnd 13-23: Sc in each st around.
Rnd 24: Sc in each st around, join with sl st in first st. Fasten off.

Body & Head

Rnd 1: With **Light brown**. Hold legs together with upper inner thighs together and toes pointed forwards. Insert hook in the center on innermost thigh of first leg, pull out the loop from second leg, ch 1, sc in same st (do not count this st just for connecting legs together), sc in next 10 sts on second leg (mark first st), sc in next 10 sts on first leg. (20)

* See diagram of how to connect legs together on page 44.*

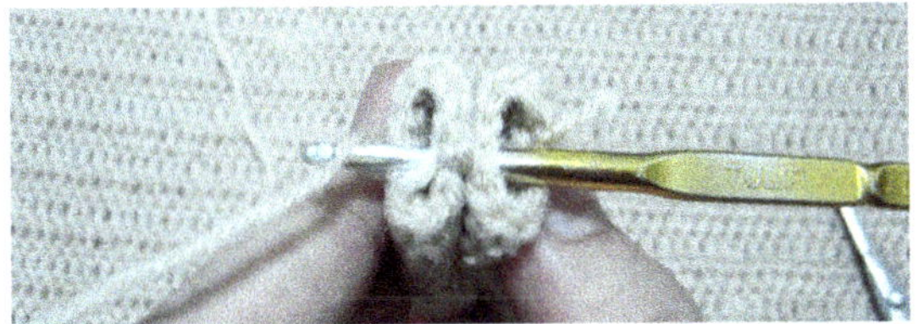

Rnd 2: (Sc in next 4 sts, 2 sc in next st) around. (24)
Rnd 3: (Sc in next 3 sts, 2 sc in next st) around. Stuff legs. (30)
Rnd 4-6: Sc in each st around.
Rnd 7: Sc in each st around, changing to **Yellow** in last 2 loops of last st.
Rnd 8: (Sc in next 3 sts, sc next 2 sts tog) around. (24)
Rnd 9: Working in back loops only. Sc in each st around.
Rnd 10-14: Sc in each st around.
Rnd 15: (Sc in next 2 sts, sc next 2 sts tog) around. Stuff. (18)
Rnd 16: (Sc next 2 sts tog, sc in next st) around, changing to **Light brown** in last 2 loops of last st. (12)
Rnd 17: (Sc in next st, 2 sc in next st) around. Stuff. (18)
Rnd 18: (2 sc in next st, sc in next 2 sts) around. (24)
Rnd 19: (Sc in next 3 sts, 2 sc in next st) around. (30)
Rnd 20-26: Sc in each st around.
Rnd 27: (Sc in next 3 sts, sc next 2 sts tog) around. (24)
Rnd 28: (Sc next 2 sts tog, sc in next 2 sts) around. Stuff. (18)
Rnd 29: (Sc in next st, sc next 2 sts tog) around. (12)
Rnd 30: (Sc next 2 sts tog) around, join with sl st in first st. Fasten off. (6)

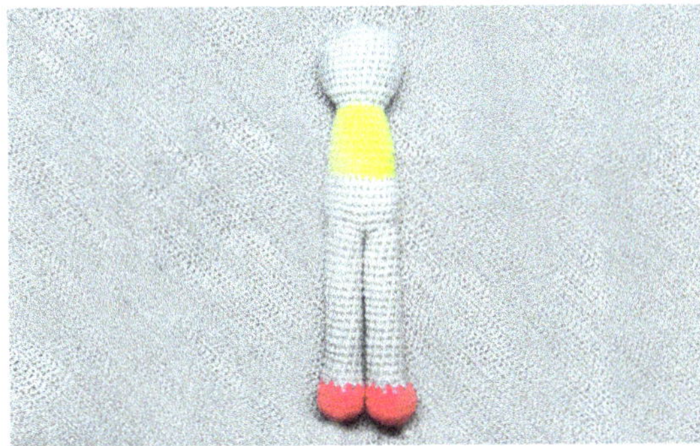

Skirt

Rnd 1: Join **Red** yarn to free loop of rnd 8 of the body, ch 3 (count as one st), 2 dc in same st, 3 dc in next st around, join with sl st in first st. (72)
Rnd 2: Ch 3, dc in same st, 2 dc in next st around, join with sl st in first st. (144)

Rnd 3: Working in front loops only, ch 1, sc in same st, (ch 3, sc in next st) around, join with sl st in first st, fasten off.

Rnd 4: Working in back loops of rnd 2 only. Join **Orange** yarn to back loop of rnd 2, ch 3, dc in each st around, join with sl st in first st.

Rnd 5: Ch 3, dc in each st around, join with sl st in first st.

Rnd 6: Working in front loops only, ch 1, sc in same st, (ch 3, sc in next st) around, join with sl st in first st, fasten off.

Rnd 7: Working in back loops of rnd 5 only. Join **Yellow** to back loop of rnd 5, ch 3, dc in each st around, join with sl st in first st.

Rnd 8: Ch 3, dc in each st around, join with sl st in first st.

Rnd 9: Working in front loops only, ch 1, sc in same st, (ch 3, sc in next st) around, join with sl st in first st, fasten off.

Rnd 10: Working in back loops of rnd 8 only. Join **Green** yarn to back loop of rnd 8, ch 3, dc in each st around, join with sl st in first st.

Rnd 11: Ch 3, dc in each st around, join with sl st in first st.

Rnd 12: Working in front loops only, ch 1, sc in same st, (ch 3, sc in next st) around, join with sl st in first st, fasten off.

Rnd 13: Working in back loops of rnd 11 only. Join **Blue** to back loop of rnd 11, ch 3, dc in each st around, join with sl st in first st.

Rnd 14: Ch 3, dc in each st around, join with sl st in first st.

Rnd 15: Working in front loops only, ch 1, sc in same st, (ch 3, sc in next st) around, join with sl st in first st, fasten off.

Rnd 16: Working in back loops of rnd 14 only. Join **Dark blue** yarn to back loop of rnd 14, ch 3, dc in each st around, join with sl st in first st.

Rnd 17: Ch 3, dc in each st around, join with sl st in first st.

Rnd 18: Working in front loops only, ch 1, sc in same st, (ch 3, sc in next st) around, join with sl st in first st, fasten off.

Rnd 19: Working in back loops of rnd 17 only. Join **Purple** yarn to back loop of rnd 17, ch 3, dc in each st around, join with sl st in first st.

Rnd 20-21: Ch 3, dc in each st around, join with sl st in first st.

Rnd 22: Ch 1, sc in same st, (ch 3, sc in next st) around, join with sl st in first st, fasten off.

Arm

Make 2, only stuff top of arm (rnds 1-4).

Rnd 1: With **Yellow**, ch 2, 6 sc in second chain from hook. (6)

Rnd 2: 2 sc in each st around. (12)

Rnd 3: Sc in each st around.

Rnd 4: (Sc next 2 sts tog, sc in next 2 sts) around, changing to **Light brown** in last 2 loops of last st. Stuff. (9)

Rnd 5: Working in back loops only. (Sc in next st, sc next 2 sts tog) 3 times. (6)

Rnd 6-10: Sc in each st around.

Rnd 11: For thumb, 2 sc in first st, skip next 4 sts, 2 sc in next st, join with sl st in first st. Fasten off.

Rnd 11: For hand, Join **Light brown** yarn to next free st on rnd 10, ch 1, 2 sc in same st, (2 sc in next st) 3 times.(8)

Rnd 12: Sc in each st around. (8)

Row 13: Working in rows, flatten last rnd, matching sts and working through both thicknesses, sc in next 2 sts, sl st in next st. Fasten off.

Row 13				cxx		
Rnd 12		xx	xx	xx	xx	
Rnd 11	v	v	v	v	v	v
Rnd 10	x	x	x	x	x	x

Pink = hand

Black = thumb

x = sc

v = 2 sc in same st

c = slip stitch

Sleeves

Join **Yellow** yarn to free loop on rnd 4, ch 1, sc in same st, (ch 3, sc in next st) around, join with sl st in first st. Fasten off.
Sew arms to body on rnds 14-15 with thumbs towards front.

Hair

Rnd 1: With **Dark brown**, ch 2, 6 sc in second ch from hook. (6)
Rnd 2: 2 sc in each st around. (12)
Rnd 3: (Sc in next st, 2 sc in next st) around. (18)
Rnd 4: (Sc in next 2 sts, 2 sc in next st) around. (24)
Rnd 5 : (Sc in next 3 sts, 2 sc in next st) around. (30)
Row 6: Working in rows. Ch 10, sc in second ch from hook, sc in next 8 chs, sc in next st, ch 15, sc in second ch from hook, sc in next 13 chs, sc in next st, (ch 20, sc in second ch from hook, sc in next 18 chs, sc in next st) 17 times, ch 15, sc in second ch from hook, sc in next 13 chs, sc in next st, ch 10, sc in second ch from hook, sc in next 8 chs, sc in next st. Leave long end for sewing, fasten off.

Pin hair on head and sew.

Flower

Make 9 (Make one each in Red, Orange, Purple, Blue and Dark blue. Make two each in Yellow and Green).
Ch 4, sl st in first ch*, (ch 3, sl st in first ch*) 4 times, fasten off.
*same chain, the first starting chain.

Pin flowers around head as shown in pictures. Sew flowers on head with white beads in the middle of flowers.

Finishing

Sew eyes 4 sts apart between rnds 23-24 of head. With **Black** embroidery floss, embroider eyelashes. With **Red**, embroider mouth.

How to join Yarn.

Join yarn to free loop, ch 1, sc in same st.

How to read pattern.

Rnd 4: (Sc in next 2 sts, 2 sc in next st) around. (24)

Number (24) at the end of round = number of stitches after finished round.

Rnd 5: (Sc in next 3 sts, 2 sc in next st) around. (30)

Repeat (Sc in next 3 sts, 2 sc in next st) until end of round

=> Rnd 5: (Sc in next 3 sts, 2 sc in next st), (Sc in next 3 sts, 2 sc in next st), (Sc in next 3 sts, 2 sc in next st), (Sc in next 3 sts, 2 sc in next st), (Sc in next 3 sts, 2 sc in next st), (Sc in next 3 sts, 2 sc in next st)

Total stitches of Rnd 5 = 5+5+5+5+5+5 = 30 sts

Rnd 6: Sc in next 2 sts, 2 sc in next st, (sc in next 4 sts, 2 sc in next st) 5 times, sc in next 2 sts. (36)

Repeat (sc in next 4 sts, 2 sc in next st) 5 times

=> Rnd 6: Sc in next 2 sts, 2 sc in next st, (sc in next 4 sts, 2 sc in next st), (sc in next 4 sts, 2 sc in next st), (sc in next 4 sts, 2 sc in next st), (sc in next 4 sts, 2 sc in next st), (sc in next 4 sts, 2 sc in next st), sc in next 2 sts.

Total stitches of Rnd 6 = 2+2+6+6+6+6+6+2 = 36 sts

Comparison color chart for Catania & DMC Petra No3

Color	Catania	DMC Petra No3
cream	130	ECRU
red	115	5321
black	110	5310
white	106	B5200
light pink	246	54461
pink	222	54458
apple green	205	5907
jade	253	53814
green	241	5905
light brown	248	5712
purple	240	53837
light blue	173	54518
blue	247	5798
dark blue	164	5823
yellow	208	5745
orange	189	5608
dark brown	162	5938
light green	385	5772
taupe	254	5646

Hair

If you use these yarns: DMC Petra No 3, Robin DK or Sirdar Hayfield Bonus DK you can split it into 3 thin strands .

Bride & Groom patterns split yarn into 3 thin strands and follow the instructions for the hair as when you use 4 ply yarn.

Cute couple patterns: split yarn into 3 thin strands and use 2 thin strands instead of 1 strand. The instructions for the hair are the same as when you use 4 ply yarn.

Yarn Weight System

USA		UK	Australia	Recommended Hook in Metric (mm)
0 lace	Lace weight	1 ply	2 ply	1.5 - 2.25 mm
1 superfine	Fingering	2 ply	3 ply	2.25 - 3 mm
	Sock	3 ply	3 ply	2.25 - 3.5 mm
2 fine	Sport	4 ply	5 ply	3.5 - 4.5 mm
3 light	DK Light worsted	DK	8 ply	4.5 - 5.5 mm
4 medium	Worsted	Aran	10 ply	5.5 - 6.5 mm
5 bulky	Bulky	Chunky	12 ply	6.5 - 9 mm
6 super bulky	Super Bulky	Super Chunky	14 ply	9 mm and larger

Crochet Hook Size Conversion

Hook in Metric (mm)	USA	UK	Japanese
2.00 mm	--	14	2/0
2.25 mm	B/1	13	3/0
2.50 mm	--	12	4/0
2.75 mm	C/2	--	--
3.00 mm	--	11	5/0
3.25 mm	D/3	10	--
3.50 mm	E/4	9	6/0
3.75 mm	F/5	--	--
4.00 mm	G/6	8	7/0
4.50 mm	7	7	7.5/0
5.00 mm	H/8	6	8/0
5.50 mm	I/9	5	--
6.00 mm	J/10	4	10/0
6.50 mm	K/10.5	3	7

Follow Sayjai on www.facebook.com/kandjdolls.amigurumi.patterns

or kandjdolls.blogspot.com for new ideas & patterns

Copyright

First Edition
Date of publication: 25th of February 2015
Editor: Robert Appelboom
Publisher: K and J Publishing
Cambridge, England

This is the fourth volume in "Sayjai's Amigurumi Crochet Patterns" series.
Below are volume 1, 2 and 3 which can be ordered at your local or online bookstore:

Easy Amigurumi
Subtitle: 28 doll patterns
Publisher: K and J Publishing
Author: Sayjai Thawornsupacharoen
Publication date: 18th of July 2014
ISBN: 978-1910407011

Huggy Dolls Amigurumi
Subtitle: 15 Huggable Doll Patterns
Publisher: K and J Publishing
Author: Sayjai Thawornsupacharoen
Publication date: 14th of June 2014
ISBN: 978-1910407028

Dress Up Dolls Amigurumi
Subtitle: 5 big dolls with clothes, shoes, accessories, tiny bear and big carry bag patterns
Publisher: K and J Publishing
Author: Sayjai Thawornsupacharoen
Publication date: 27th of September 2014
ISBN: 978-1910407066

www.ingramcontent.com/pod-product-compliance
Ingram Content Group UK Ltd.
Pitfield, Milton Keynes, MK11 3LW, UK
UKHW050141280726
14058UKWH00006B/764

9 781910 407189